AF293504

Maher Asaad Baker

Nordic Folk

ISBN Softcover: 978-3-384-36115-8

ISBN Hardback: 978-3-384-36116-5

ISBN E-Book: 978-3-384-36117-2

Cover image designed by Freepik

Contents

Introduction

Nordic folk music can be considered as the traditional, or more precisely 1900 music from Nordic countries Denmark, Norway, Sweden, Finland and Iceland. It is in this music that one can get to notice the cultures and histories of the northernmost countries of Europe. As folk music is one of the art forms that are associated with geography, rural areas, ancestors, and history, Nordic folk music contains a wide range of Nordic societies' perspectives of otherness and sameness across centuries.

Nordic Folk Music is a style of music that features primarily folk instruments and for the vocals, people instead of using other instruments.

Folk music of the Nordic countries was likely generated before even recorded music could be produced since it was a kind of communal music that was passed through generations of a given culture. Nordic folk music is characterized by several key qualities: Some features, that can be attributed to Nordic folk music, are the following:

-        Literary/Localized/native/native language/tribal/area-specific chants or lyricized tunes.

- Sometimes, even the author is not known, or it is an assembly of authors at some stage in time.

- A link to work, festivity and other business.

- Preference for definite tools like fiddle, accordion and willow flutes

- For example, staccato, legato, modal scales or rhythms, which are in some way shaped by an accentuation of language.

- Swan "...song lyrics from the culture myth and personification of daily life"

This type of music was used for social uses and these included dancing, a celebration of season, a rite of passage, leisure as well as change of status throughout the life cycle. The performers were from families and villages, not those who were musicians who were selling concerts or records. One person could write the first sentence or the first tunes, which were then handed down and in various forms, changed in many generations of oral history and variation, leading to many forms of regional and idiosyncratic song. All this and the overall anonymity of the Northern area make it almost impossible to establish where, precisely, these given Nordic folk songs stem from. However, their relevance up to the present day proves that folk music is capable of reflecting the key features of Nordic people's identity for centuries.

Several related factors indicate why folk music has always played an important role in reflecting a positive image of the self among the Nordic people. First, it connects the people of present-day Nordic with their pre-historic and cultural backgrounds which existed even before the use of urban and modern means of recording their existence and progress, at least for a couple of hundred years. The songs are a portrayal of life as it entailed the farmers who were fishes, the forest dwellers, the first inhabitants of the nutrient-rich Nordic lands and those who lived in synch with nature and its rhythmic cycles.

Secondly, folk music also continued to be the fundament for the majority of modern Nordic pop music as well. It can be said that folk motifs and stories go on transforming into new images in the rock, jazz and electronic styles up to the present day. As it consciously or not the young Nordic musicians in this genre 'cross over' folk traditions into the songwriting techniques, intervals and moods of the modern music.

Last, at the geo-political dimension, the folk music of Nordic countries plays an essential role in strengthening sustainable cultural diplomacy between the currently affiliated Nordic countries. For instance, there is some evidence that cross-cultural export co-operation in Nordic folk music has increased in the last decades. The findings indicate that most of the formal cultural activities are directed towards folk music hence exchange programs, concerts, youth engagement and archiving. This all serves to maintain the ongoing building and marketing of Copenhagen, Stockholm and Oslo as creative and sustainable capitals informed and drawing on tradition. While traditions tend to become multicultural in the world under the globalization processes, the transmitted folk arts are more important to maintain the specific tendencies of the Nordic societies' cultures in the global space.

Nordic folk music remains vitally important within contemporary Nordic societies, it can be stated that the concept of Nordic folk music persists as culturally significant in today's Nordic societies by:

- Bringing today's Nordic people their ancestors and Ethnicity

- Interacting new forms of rhythms inherent in the classic folk music of the Nordic countries into popular music styles

- Sharing experiences and policy practices to promote the cultural identity in the Nordic countries.

- Preserving dear familiarity with rituals distinct for the Nordic countries and different from the rest of the globe.

Because Nordic folk music arose from the rural peoples' culture of social gatherings, this tradition must carry the main historical archaic evolution trends of the Nordic societies of the last thousand years. While every country in the Nordics has it own regional folk music that can be probably associated with the geography, economy, events, mythology, etc of the country there are some common features one might observe.

Before the thousand AD, Nordic music was of simpler types and was closer to the earth and was founded on the tribal beliefs of the shamans. Medieval Nordic instrumentation started somewhere between 1000-1500AD and included fiddles, flutes, as well as animal horns. This is connected with the rise of pastoralism like sheep farming, the disappearance of heathenry as a form of relation to the wild through pagan rituals concerning the Black Plague, the dominance of the church and the rise of the early mercantile economy.

From 1500 to 1800 CE the Nordic folk music began to become more distinct from one another, attributed mainly to the breakdown of the Kalmar Union and the changes brought by the Reformation. Today, hymnal repertoires and animating patriotism with the songs contribute to the creation of specifically Norwegian, Swedish, Danish and Finnish song collections. Through enhanced contacts with continental Europe and Britain dance forms and instruments such as the viol were introduced. The represented market economy, the printing press and the rather early industrialization supported the collecting, publishing, and formalization of regional oral folk music.

Finally, the processes of urbanization, nationalism and mass media during the 19th and the 20th centuries in the Nordic countries directed the audience's attention to the revival of the folklore. Collections of folk songs made by nations – Like 'Kalevala' of Finland and concert performances and urban dance societies made the routine of folk songs as symbols of nationalism. The nationalist classical music was engaged by Nordic composers who also contributed folklore motives to it. After the sixties, new waves of culture standardization and globalization reawakened traditions of folk culture collection and propagated by relics and regulation. This proved true by bringing them back to the forefront of themes incorporated into rocks, this electronic, and jazz fusion.

It's somehow daunting to see how those young Nordic artists have still to be given this immensely complex and continuously developing musical armor – shamanistic prehistoric art, medieval struggle, imperial decline, nationalism, industrial and post-industrial post-modern globalization. Songs, therefore, are semiotically coded with other layers of historical meanings and represent the processes involved in the management of the tensions between globalization and the particularism within Nordic music in music.

Nordic folk music is therefore intrinsically linked socio-culturally to historical political narratives as well as sociocultural folkloric myths, historical and fictional Nordic stories and real-lived Nordic regional practices typical of generations. As a non-literary narrative or entertainment, the content reflects how rural families and communities of fishermen, subsistence farmers, reindeer herders and craftsmen entertained themselves and disseminated information and elaborated their winters, often in isolation, until the process of urbanization.

Shamanic chants as well as drumming are the oldest form of Nordic folk music that has been performed only by revival bands of modern times like that from Norway – Wardruna. These pre-historic cultures had their spirituality in animism, ancestor worship and Norse pantheons in song, the beauty, hooligans and riddles of the Norse wilderness. Epics like the Finnish 'Kalevala' belong to pre-Christian polytheism and belong to the area of epic songs about magic, chaos, death, and cosmogony.

Folk music addressed Christianity in parallel and opposition to other types of Norse and other kinds of Nordic paganisms for several centuries after they diminished. singing of sacred church music or simple hymns in praising God with rousing secular tunes and country dance for other celebrations like saint's days or weddings on the same village streets. According to the church, such practices as drumming, jumping dances and fiddles were promoting immoral conduct. Hymns and religious scriptures morality together with some popular tunes follow the tones and the awakened generations helped to clean music over the generations. Sacred compositions sung and played in pilgrimages ensured that people relating throughout lengthy and tiresome trips on foot were able to form fellowship. Hence, the relationships between Nordic folk music and religious features also developed when society went through centuries.

In addition to the cosmic mythical level, there are popular folk songs in the Nordic area that are more obvious in connection with the community. There were songs to be sung in Viking longships and this was used to facilitate rhythm among the rowers. While blowing of horns and calling helped to bring together animals for transhumance across large areas of the highland grazing fields. In this sense, the social concern from women is signified from the vocal cries of the chores at home to the rhymes of the children with babies. North Atlantic fishermen of diverse fishing and whaling groups that convened on the shores of Nordic countries sang shanties while working in coordination in the hostile and dangerous sea.

Songs and dancing were done during specific periods in the year for instance during summer solstice or the Christmas period or even during harvest. Lamentation songs offered consolation to the deceased's kin and dancing songs promoted courting during the Nordic funerals or weddings as well as saint festivity periods. The heroic re-creation of significant characters and events includes ballads that depict famines, battles, or disasters that form part of the history of attack, hunger, resistance, or grief of a community. Besides, shorter lyric verses also encompassed nearly all aspects of life such as desire, betrayal, foolishness, love, forgiveness, foolishness, patriotism, bravery, loneliness and grief. Song was as much a part of the belt-and-suspenders Nordic existence at all strata from the rake's progress to the peasant's pauper.

Again, as with most folk song's words stretch only part of the truth and when it comes to Nordic countries it would be remiss not to mention the beautiful instrumental tunes and dances that are done in accompaniment to the songs and which are as much a gateway into the traditional Nordic pastimes as the lyrics themselves.

Of course, every animal, plant and other natural substance that can be found in the Nordic villages and rural forests was used as musical material. It is done by covering the drums with reindeer and cattle skins. Bones shake within flutes. This is done by the blacksmiths where the tuned steel bars are played percussively. Violins and wooden horns come from a pool of production from the Norden timber reserve. The willow flutes from whistle pipes to the säckpipa bagpipe and all of the instruments only use hollow willow reeds which are rare and can only be sourced in northern locations. For horn sound fish air bladders expand like balloons. Fiddle strings are either made of horsehair or woven catgut. Waulking boards are used to beaten during the finishing of linen fabrics. Water musical instruments make the sounds by blowing musical notes through water. Seabird wings produce a whistling sound when the wings are twirled through the air. Hence Nordic music cultures adequately benefitted from each acoustical possibility of a solitary cold climate biome. They do that still today in neo-folk music revivals.

There is also a clear link between dancing and musical genres by hundreds of named Nordic set dances for couples or groups. Some of the folk dances of the present time originated from the medieval European dance forms while others originated from Pagan rings. To this day, there are short competitive solo dances for example Norwegian halling or in Sweden polska. Folk couples still move to fiddles and accordions and communities round up the festive seasons with a circle dance like their forefathers did generations back. The dances thus transmit kinetic generational memory as the melodies the lyrics or the words do also.

Consequently, Nordic folk music is a tremendous sphere of traditional song, sound, and dance that can immediately tie the contemporary Nordic creation to the centuries before the beginning of music recording. It throbs with the metronomic rhythms which have been pulling the strings of the Nordic societies while the culture changed for 10 centuries.

Beginning with ancient shamanic and Norse mythological roots, moving through medieval focus on rurality and Christianity, all the way up to the modern trends of urbanization, technological advancement, and globalization, Nordic folk arts keep and restore the reflections of the fundamental guidelines of how to inhabit these northernmost regions of Europe. The music, therefore, has embedded and simultaneously, has multiple historical significations and enactments of Nordic selves in a perpetually varying process of performing local differences against a backdrop of globalization homogeneity.

Nordic folk music therefore remains a highly flexible but grounded cultural product that has entered the 21st century still afloat and largely unscathed. Thus, the continuous practice of folk music in every period of the Nordic countries corresponds to the current requirement of the contemporary Nordic countries, which aim to brand their capitals as creative cities of the globalized modern world, while still preserving the Nordic cultural identity as a valuable asset. Many tools have shifted on the Nordic shores for centuries, but the songs remain to sing.

The Foundations

Music has always been an important aspect of the lives of people within the Nordic countries including Denmark, Finland, Iceland, Norway, and Sweden. Social factors, which include geographical location, climatic conditions and previous experiences have also influenced the music of the region which has similar tones but is rich in variation because each country has its unique style.

This is a small part of the entire early Nordic Music that originated from the native people of the region known as Sami and the other part was from the successive waves of immigrants and settlers who came to live within the region. Namely, due to long winters and the relative isolation of rural communities developed gradually old songs and customs, appearing at the same time the regional styles. The formation of the Nordic countries as independent nation-states between the 16th and 19th centuries brought the emergence of proto-European definitions and categorizations to an area that remains in the process of defining a specific ethnic and cultural identity even today secondly it is important to recognize that even as the development of Nordic music became increasingly influenced by the larger European tradition, it also influenced in turn, European music.

The first level of indigenous music of Nordic countries would be the Sami people who are the native inhabitants of northern Norway, Sweden and Finland and some parts of Russia known by the name of Lapland. The Sami people are believed to have migrated to northern Scandinavia to participate in the rearing of reindeer during about 3000 BCE. In terms of individual songs, their music imitates natural and animal sounds and includes joiks: vocal chants and luohti; herding calls for lavlu: yoik-like songs. With the help of relics, it can be concluded that during the fiestas of seasons and religious activities, people were involved in singing and dancing which were supported by rhythm sticks, drums, flutes and stringed instruments. Sami music was a basis on which other cultures of Scandinavia proceeded and contained elements that are found in the Nordic folk songs of today.

From the 8th to the 12th centuries CE, Nordic music was primarily monophonic, a single melody line without harmonic support in the Christian religious chants that were brought in by monks and priests who were converting the pagans. Song ranges were confined up to five notes; texts borrowed from Latin sacred literature, and only percussive accompaniments, if any, were used. A lot of them had special sad intonations, which can be characteristic of further Nordic folklore traditions. There is not much written evidence that gives accurate descriptions of how the early Nordic monophonic sounded like.

There are more cheerful dance music and ballads for communal events after the Black Death occurred in Scandinavia in the 14th century but for the polyphonic, it continued as monophonic. These pointed to a shift in focus to music for entertainment apart from religion and cults and rites. Through the performances of minstrels as well as traveling singers, songs all over Europe were sung; formatted with aspects of storytelling and poetry in songs. Some of them include regionalism which stems from native folk songs that were learned by the members of the rural communities by word of mouth across generations.

The beats of today's recognizable Nordic instruments were popular and embraced as accompaniments for the folk partials and the vocals by the 1500s. Some of these are the Norwegian fiddle known as the hardingfele, the Swedish keyed fiddle also known as the nyckelharpa and the Finnish zither also referred to as the kantele was used for dance tunes for weddings and other ceremonies, poetic songs, calls for shepherds and work songs. The wooden flutes, the willow pipe horns known as säckpipa, the jaw harps, the ancient lutes, the primitive fiddles which were known as the talharpa, and the Swedish bagpipes also got more popularity for folk performances.

Besides, dancing was probable after these instrumental and vocal compositions. In the Nordic group parishes, there were festive non-professional dances like the Swedish Polska, the Norwegian springar, and the Danish gammeldans that entertained the rural folks during the holidays and also acted as marketplaces for marriages for the youth of ages. Consequently, the dances appeared to belong to the region; while there were Swedish dances of duple meter, there were Norwegian dances in triple meter. For example, the folk instruments and the asymmetrical musical rhythms that characterize the dance numbers propagated such genres of music in the Nordic countries.

Following the spread of Gutenberg's printing press which started in the 1500s, strolling actors and entertainers had an ease of spreading printed folk ballads and dance songs at fairs and this saw the popularization of the oral history which was put in a form that could be read then performed over and over again. Because of this, it promoted the standardization of musical practices within the Nordic society, while at the same time enabling a quicker switch between with faster means of dissemination between the different settlements hence strengthening of the regional styles. Their popular tunes were in forms that any average musician in the village could play as opposed to the Church musician and the itinerant minstrels.

Thus, despite the general tendencies in the formation of the song repertoire, each country had its own national color. For instance, Danish legends were based on tragic stories where as Swedish ones were in the form of song and dance. Songs spread between countries as well, with many traipsing back and forth across borders: Danish and Swedish folk tunes show that more than one-third of them are borrowed between them. With growing literacy and printed distributed in the society and continuing oral tradition during 18th century, Nordic folk music peaked in terms of popularity and standardization.

University students in the early nineteenth century across the Scandinavian region formed nationalist groups with the aim of achieving cultural nationalism in their respective countries. Folklor and music from indigenous languages were at the core of these movements as cultural representations that transcended the social class divide. Ethnographers and musicians gathered disappearing pastoral tunes by conversing with rural farmers and choosing harmonies considered as authentic national tunes free from external influence.

For instance, Norwegian composer Ludvig Mathias Lindeman travelled around the countryside of Telemark in the 1840s and 1850s collecting surviving traditional melodies that may soon be lost due to changing lifestyles brought about by industrialisation. He released collections such as Ældre og nyere norske Fjeldmelodier (Old and New Norwegian Mountain Melodies) in which he disseminated popular folk tunes like "Solveig's Song" to a new broader public so as to popularize them as symbols of the Norwegian people. Parallel processes in other

Scandinavian countries were equally purposeful in amplifying romantic folk music as the essence of the nation while deleting the foreign-oriented ones.

This kind of nationalist adulation of so-called folk purity impacted the primarily classical composers from Edvard Grieg to Jean Sibelius where the orchestral scores were laden with folk motifs for romanticism projected as cultural authenticity. In turn, their internationally celebrated works transplanted Swedish polska beats, Norwegian Hardanger fiddle styles, and Finnish Karelian vocables, and transformed them into defining Nordic sounds. Although it is not typical of the tradition, this synthesis made the more extensive public aware of the Nordic music style.

Having experienced mass emigration to North America in mid mid-1800s meant people moved with their beloved folk items to the new society. About 1. About 3 million Swedes immigrated to America in the period between 1850 and 1930s, as well as several hundreds of thousands of their closest neighbors, mainly for new homestead establishments as farmers or tradespeople in the Upper Middle western states such as Minnesota, Wisconsin, Michigan, Iowa, and the Dakotas. Patriotic of preserving cultural traditions in their rather strange new world, the Scandinavian settlers started forming township dance clubs, regional fiddling, choral societies and academic repositories like the Norwegian-American Historical Association, periodicals and producing folk music entertainment for the next generations of Nordic immigrants through regional Scandinavian music festivals.

In these reciprocal processes, the European string band and dance genre that migrants encountered in rural North America by no means ceased to affect the Nordic tunes back in the old world dispatched across the sea. It also gave the continuous evolution of other more developing national folk forms across the Atlantic passage transference.

As urbanization, which was the result of industrialization, took place during the later part of the nineteenth and twentieth century, the rural society was 'shrinking', so the folk tradition which had been passed from generation to generation for centuries was exposed in a more confined way. Workers flocked to factories in cities for jobs, and Americanization in the form of jazz, rock and pop pushed reels and ballads to the sides in radio. When the late generation was gone, folk music was in danger of being lost and that was a reason for concern.

However, the legal action of the foreign countries to preserve the musical heritage of the Scandinavians continued through the academic and creative performances to the posterity. In workshops of Hardanger fiddle of Norway, the playedance movement of Sweden, which is a revival gammeldansen traditions, folk dance Danish, folk dancing tournaments and spelemannslag or fiddler clubs' students maintained folk instruments and folk songs as integral elements of national character. Such state institutions as archives, museums, festivals, instructional resources and youth education funded folk arts for while such practices were fast becoming irrelevant, they were preserved.

The most successful attempt, as it seems, occurred in the early seventies with the Nordic folk wave when youth picked their roots but translated them into the seventies and beyond feel with the roots of the structure intact. Young bands and artists from the Nordic countries, such as Filarfolket from Sweden, Bukkene Bruse from Norway, Dreamers' Circus from Denmark, and Frigg of Finland representative of the fresh talents bringing youthful vitality into what is essentially classical music and classical instruments through the creation of their new albums and concept live shows. Some described the delightful, even playful spirit of hundreds if not thousands of years of Nordic folklore creativity that could seem to have been alive today if only people would let it. Intending to take people back to life and at the same time question the folk genre, they have made a positive input towards folk music's sustained relevance up to the 21st century.

For more than a thousand years after the first basilisks of the frozen north the wind of Scandinavia hums with history and is looking forward with happy anticipation. And while with time the ornaments may shift Nordic music has remained entirely loyal to its independent gloom, quizzical optimism for the next generation, and more unexplored potential.

The folk music of Nordic has genes that go down generations and share cultural instruments and vocals and dances that are unique to the region. Classical Nordic folk music and characteristics of the field are the Hardanger fiddle, nyckelharpa, and jouhikko. The wailing stringed instruments contrast with regional singing techniques from simple melodic lines to the specific Swedish calls to come, the kulning. All these stems from basic folk dances which begin with Polska up to the hambo which all feature distinct rhythms and movement patterns.

Norway, Sweden, Finland, Iceland and Denmark were geographically isolated in both farmsteads and fishing villages and over many generations, these regional folk styles quite naturally developed. Indigenous characteristics of any certain area also affected instruments that is: Indigenous materials on indigenous instruments&& There was also creative vocalism and dancing due to long winters. Several parts shifted across cultures but, far-off cities came up with their unique brand images. While many societies of most of the Nordic countries are integrated into the modern world, many societies keep folk crafts alive through pride through the means of festivals, competitions, schools, and organizations.

It has invariably been the stringed family which forms the basis of the folk music of the Nordic countries, the most well-known of which is the Norwegian Hardanger fiddle. Other noteworthy contributions to the group of Nordic bowed instruments come from Sweden – nyckelharpa, and Finland – jouhikko. Even though some theories link some of the utensils to the medieval and Renaissance periods, the majority of the objects in question were manufactured in distant Nordic farms in the 16th and 18th centuries.

One of the most popular instruments of Norwegian folk music is the Hardanger fiddle which emerged in the Hardanger region in West Norway. The Hardanger fiddle (hardingfele) remains a European violin that is envisaged with extra sub-judges or what is commonly referred to as the sympathetic strings that are located below the main bridge. These resonators give off a resonating sound that has been said to be similar to the sound made by waterfalls within the mountainous terrain of this place. Hardanger also has very elaborate pearlwork and designs on the body of the instrument and the designs on head plates.

The beginning of the Hardanger fiddles is said to have started around the middle of the seventeenth century. It began to spread to areas and regions other than the Hardanger farmlands and by the close of the 19th century had become the national fiddle of Norway. The last pieces which became the characteristic elements, the understrings are known to have been added to the kantele in 1800's by the folk musician Myllarguten.

Today the Hardanger style so endemic to the Norwegian tradition of fiddle music goes on to announce more global significance. The above-given rosin profiles depict the connection of the Hardanger fiddle with the Norwegian identity from family parties to the orchestra. Competition and schools today ensure that the tradition is passed on to the next generations to avoid the culture dying out.

In Sweden probably the most popular folk instrument stems not from the frigid Arctic tundra of Samiland but from the Sunnansj woods and mines. It is also called the keyed fiddle; the nyckelharpa may have been developed when minstrels demanded a portable version of the church organs. NACKTBLÅS of the early period of the 13th century was the bow-stringed instrument as well as a keyboard.

Nonetheless, nyckelharpas are known to have attained their fuller development under what can be referred to as the 'great' instrument makers of the Sunnansjö area at the same time as the improvement in iron-making technology in the early 16th and the 17th centuries. Some of these techniques such as chromatic tuning keys are still in use today in the nyckelharpas and were developed by professional players like Sand Hans Ersson (1632-1708). Nyckelharpas were there up to the 1700s; they were present in central Sweden in the 1800s.

But with the rise of industrialization, there was a high rate of people moving from the rural areas hence reduced populations and the nyckelharpas being almost extinct by the start of the 20th century. A revival process started in the 1970s because of artists like Eric Sahlström. Today the nyckelharpa is an instrument that represents Swedish folk domestically and internationally through SSR.

Finns also have the jouhikko older than the Norwegian Hardanger dating back to Vikings. Said to derive from still older forms of lyre and lure, the Jouhikko originated among Finland's marginal west coast fishing communities in the twelfth to fourteenth centuries. These early single-string jouhikanteles were later given two and three strings in addition to the arched bridge and beautiful scrollwork.

Regional jouhikko styles evolved until 19th-century political processes launched attempts to make Finns embrace Russian and Swedish identities. However, the national epic Kalevala collected in the nineteenth century revived the Finns and their culture. Such masters as Sakari Ilomäki (1885-1964) made jouhikko survive the chaos to become the modern Finnish national instrument.

Jouhikkos now bring historical Finness to provincial fairs and even avant-garde pieces on the international level. Active schools are educating new generations to pull jouhikkos as a living symbol of valued cultural legacy.

It is just as the geographical origins of the instruments influenced the tones of their music, so the Nordic landscapes and occupations imbued folk vocals with their unique character. It is crucial to understand that vocalizing styles are not arbitrary; there are origins in Norwegian cattle calls and Finnish epic poetry. Voices such as the Swedish kulning herding shouts and the Danish líur singing intermingle with the sounds of nature in various forms of Scandinavian arts.

The immense forests of Sweden, remote pastures, and mountain valleys created the environment for a powerful, but tender vocal tradition inspired, paradoxically, by both powerful and tender virtues. To call together dispersed cattle while moving livestock between mountain dairy farms, herding girls sang loud, resonant calls called kuhreihen or kulning. The vocal styling involves singing in a high pitch with the additional use of shimmering harmonics, which makes the sound travel over large distances through sharp soprano tones and well-measured breaths.

These herding shouts constitute Sweden's most characteristic indigenous vocal instrument and originated at the latest in the Middle Ages in connection with the spread of transhumant pastoralism. While the dialects of the remote regions had different ornaments, kulning was the cultural link between Swedes from Dalarna and Gotland. As late as the 19th century printed notation saved characteristic calls such as locklåt that might otherwise have vanished in the age of industrialization and urbanization.

Thankfully however due to efforts made in the fight against cultural erosion kulning survives today as part of the recognized folklore of Sweden. Sung both casually and expertly nowadays, the kulning singers take time to practice the right arching posture, resonance, and control. Other collections such as Fäbodlåten spread kulning across the globe transforming it into musical production.

Epic poetry occupied one of the highest places in the ancient Finnish culture, intermixing history, myths and verse with musical performance Genres such as the Kalevala collected in the nineteenth century and the Kanteletar poetry collections compiled during the Finnish national romantic period. And the rune singing cultures of the region determined the further evolution of the stylistic and intonational processes, which combined coarse chanting and free pitch variation based on the natural speech pulse.

Finnish runic writing tradition is known to reach at least the pre-Christianity period of the first millennium. If skalds were to travel from one isolated homestead to another, they would perform mythologically based poetry called runot to the tunes of plucked kantele at occasions and celebrations. Since the ancient runes had no written language, aššu both passed down cultural history and amused. Singers memorized hundreds of poetic lines providing a level of flexibility in the recombinations that can be applied to any event or audience.

Epic rune chanting thus linked generations of Finns through a crucial and dynamic performer-audience-based oral art form. While nationalism in the nineteenth century posed the danger of a monotonous cultural sameness in the Russian and Swedish spheres, the rune verse came to form the core of the Finnish romantic arts renaissance. Today regional rune singing clubs maintain such Finnish dialects that sustain this 'sung history,' transferred through unbroken centuries.

As a bridge between, epic runic chanting and Scandinavian ballads there is a special Danish singing tradition called líur which connects narrative folk singing to the pastoral poetic culture. Herding girls' líur tunes imitate runos' falling pitch contour and a variable tempo and comprise narratives and dance and lyric songs. Skilled banter floated thick into the cow barns during the tediousness of winter.

Even the name of the band Norwegianises the intertwined vociferous call of a pasture and ballad tradition; the word líur means 'cow' in English and the free rhythm and modal tonality of the band reverberates through the Nordic countries from psalms to calls for herding cattle. However, because líur adopted the narrative approach which is making a constant switch between the major and parallel minor keys, it is possible to conclude that the Danish vocal persona is unique.

Líur singers today can be generally traced down from 19th-century movements for a revival of Danish culture as early as the collected songbooks from the Askov folk high school. As much as líur vocal clubs and championships have been infiltrated by pop cultural activities, there is still a special way through which the history of the society is preserved through capella singing.

While Nordic vocalization was used for purposes such as announcements across distances, singing stories, and dance was used for celebrations and festivals in Scandinavia. The regions further developed their dance melodies and dance styles which are still seen and recognized as the people's folklore to the present. The Polska is similar to the Swedish celebrations where as Danish schottish and Norwegian reinlender are still living cultures from the past to the present.

As a fiddle and pipe-dominated dance with roots in at least the 1600s, Polska is the perpetuity of the Swedes' folk legacy. Polskas proved appropriate in providing tunes for social functions in the villages for example the fairs, church festivals, weddings, and a harvest thanksgiving with the barn dances and merry-making. People dance in couples in the manner of Polska through the medium of 3⁄4 time fiddling music.

Regardless, of whether the polkas belong to the Renaissance immigrants or some other post-Medieval era, these are firmly embedded within provincial Scandinavia to the extent that by the 1800s, Sweden had as many polka tunes as did Poland. Players from the village included Bruce, Lapp-Nils and Gagnéf; Olle made sure the Polska had become popular as the national country dance of Sweden at the close of the nineteenth century.

Waltz and fox-trot, for example, posed a threat to the Polska up to the early part of the twentieth century; however, efforts that sought to keep the Polska threatened transformed it into a valued cultural asset. The Polska tradition today is used primarily in folk music tuition and played at the majority of the popular Swedish folk music festivals including the Ransäterstämman is directly passed from one generation to the other the most typical folk dance in Sweden.

Slurred 9/8 time also characterizes Denmark's schottish that emerged at the turn of the end of the eighteenth century. Standard dance: The Schottish is kindred to the Scottish country dancing where people exhibit leaping and gliding steps well suited in to tight places as the Danish. The schottish is played at a faster tempo and, to dance the vigorous spinning of the dancers or lines, the use of the fiddle, accordion, or clarinet.

Danish nobility and salon music adopted Scottish influences but the lower strata of the

Danish society came up with the Folk schottish by the early nineteenth century. This means that practices like Christmas 'walking dances' developed from fiddlers going from door to door to performing schottish as a middle-ground between the aristocracy and the lower class of Denmark.

The schottish music written and performed by H. C. Lumbye kept the Danish Golden Age spewing more creativity into the mid-1800s. And canonical tune collections that could maintain idioms when the Schottish were no longer in the ballroom. Relatively, the blocks of waltzes and polkas increased by the 1900s while that of schottish increased as lively emblems of dear Danish folk revival arts.

One of the most popular Social Country dances in Norway originated not in Norwegian valleys but in 18 century Germany before it was brought to the isolated Norwegian towns and cities as a representative of the aristocracy. One more reignander coupling pattern was the German reignander coupling which spread along Europe as Mozart and Beethoven applied the coupling pattern in their classics. However, as reignlander forms were introduced in the country of Norway, the isolation created different strains of Norwegian reinlender ranging from the Telemark fiddle to Setesdal ganger which include street performances.

Norwegian reinlenders were not only different in texts but also music while transforming the courtly meters of the original German reignlander to folk 6/8 and 3/4 time. Faster tempo melodies were more appropriate for the Norwegian countryside dance gathering, but the partnered choreography was maintained.

Most of the tradition was fixed between 1850 and 1950 when other famous fiddlers like Knut Dahl, Eivind Groven and Hauk Buen developed precise staccato dots and passing tones.

Like the leading reinlender musicians of today, such as Daniel Sanden-Warg, these musicians seek to recover forgotten tunes and evolutions to preserve the country's dance legacy. Due to the documented support from institutions such as Oslo University and Spelemannslag support, Norwegian reinlender is preserved in two ways; formally through Spelet om Heilag Olav events and informally through Norwegian folk-dance sessions across the country.

it is possible to distinguish two major aspects of Nordic folk: the main characteristic of the people of the North could be defined as free and rather open sounding, and the melancholic attitude that the majority of the compositions express. Many of these factors are related to location and life: the snowy territories and the cold with long winters forecasted the music reflecting and longing. Midsummer was also of short nights that encouraged merry popover, wedding music and dance tunes. The culture was influenced significantly by geography as being mostly a rural, agricultural society throughout most of its history, social unfamiliarity both helped creativity yet strengthened distinct, regional dialects of the Nordic region.

Examples of what is divided by these categories include: scales include major and minor scales, mode include ionian, dorian, Phrygian and mixolydian; rhythms include quadruple, triple, time and cut-time.

In any case, most of the notes of the Nordic folk music are diatonic major and diatonic minor similar to the central European. But, Nordic folk also often use modes, specific, regular sets of whole and half tones within an octave, it sounds not so modern, it sounds more menacing. These are the Dorian and old church modes are used in songs and ballads. Modal melodies are fond of completing the phrase on any other degree than tonic scale and therefore such melodies sound uncompleted, and mysterious.

Some of the melodic patterns are also repetitive in the traditional music of the Nordic countries from the countries of the Scandinavia area. Features of the melodic and rhythmic structure of the Polish triple or compound meter are the syncopated and shift of accent to two or three beats which is normally considered to be weak. Springar also contains triple meters and bouncing of dotted rhythms, in couples, or triplets. Waltzes also appear to be featured in the Nordic areas as well In fact, there is even a dance called the Nordic Waltz. In vocal music, rhythms are therefore all-natural imitating the rhythms of speech and the metrical patterns of versification. Thus, links between downbeats and voices, or treatments of the melodies as if in dance, are drawn more narrowly than the general dynamics suggest.

Some of the most frequently reused patterns present in Nordic folk music are as follows: also a two-part song and three parts but the first part and the last part of the song have the same melody type of songs have ballad and lyric songs. Refrains and choruses with repeats can be observed in the dance songs, particularly in springars and the Portuguese polkas. Some also use what are called strophic forms in which new verses are sung to the same tune; examples of this are Danish Folk Songs and Scandinavian Sacred Songs.

Another element that has a major contribution to Nordic folk music is the variation of tones and themes as well. Imitation in the ballroom dances is also usually accompanied by changes of key between major and minor, and changes between the slower A-section melodies and the quicker B-section tunes. The other way contrast can be realized is through the change of harmony and unison melody where for instance the Hardanger fiddle has an interchange with 4 or 5 Hardanger fiddles playing the same tune. Similar patterns are also employed in the call-and-response manner in Nordic traditional music both between the singer and the choral accompaniment as well as between the solo instruments and the whole band.

Scales, rhythms, forms and contrast principles are typical for the cultures of the Nordic peoples' folk music, but each country has its regional timbre. These are local imitative styles of textiles that have been adopted through the many years of immigration into the Nordic countries. The following overview also tries to elaborate on some general characteristics of folk music in Scandinavia.

Norway: Particularly because Norway has relatively rugged geographical features, it shaped dances that are more localized as noted for instance in springar dances, the approach of vocalization is referred to as 'lydarslatter' which translates to lulling, and Hardanger fiddle. These highly resonant and usually narrow-waisted instruments are often played with the ondi and contain multiple strings and sympathetic buzzing. Norway also borrowed Polska dance forms from Sweden as well as brought in their original forms.

Sweden: typically, a strong influence of triple meter dances is seen in Swedish folk music, and shares a likeness with certain styles of central Europe; dances from Poland, Germany, or even France have been integrated with Swedish weddings and other community village dances at some point of time or the other. In general, the dances that belong to this region are the polkas – syncopated, waltzing lilts, mazurkas and schottis. Vocal music also has more P3S6 than harmony suggesting; and less VD than in Norwegian or Finnish music.

Denmark: It is a well-known fact that Danish folk have more in terms of dance music as compared to the other Nordic nations. Included are Cymbalums, clarinets, and piano violin combinations of many polkas, reels, and several jigs. Gangar circle dances, sønderhoning ("Jutland honey") lyrical formal dances and Svend Grundtvig poem singing are the forms that are much more distinguishably Danish, in contact with the more Austrian, Bohemian and German forms of the dance. Also because of past Danish choral conventions layered accompaniments and rich vocal lines are also apparent.

Finland: From slow Lapps' Sámi joiks to energetic Finnish polka dancing, it is clear that Finnish folk music is far less confined and less homogenous than its neighbours'. This area is based on elements originating from the Eastern Karelian runolaulu epic solo singing and the Western Scandinavian dance music tension between major and minor rhythm changes along with the difference between free rubato and tempo-based singing. The next two are even brighter and produce sliding tones: Kantele, which is a Finnish zither and Jouhikko, a Finnish bowed lyre.

Iceland: Last of all, in the folk one can also trace the influence of Norwegian and Celtic streaks in Iceland. Not until recent time again as a geography island, the singing style is just as distinctive as the powerful narrations although stanzas patterns are less as well. It also has complex pulses such as the 5/4, 3/4, and 4/4 'bitonal' meters, where, in this case, it means that the two layers are in different meters. All of this gives an overall impression of an eradic or, if you wish, erupting volcanic setting, which does help because most of the film was shot in Iceland.

Thus, the discussion of Nordic folk music traditions demonstrates that there is both a dense interwoven musical integration of Norway, Sweden, Denmark, Finland and Iceland and rich folk particularity within that integration. Nordic folk songs and instrumental melodies have been defined by shared scales, modes, rhythms, forms, and contrast principles. At the same time, Norwegian drones and ornamented fiddle tunes, Swedish Central European dances, Danish choruses, and island rhythms, Finnish runo singing, and Icelandic volcanic textures do not lose national colors. Regardless of different styles though, Nordic folk music's emotive characteristic reflects the Nordic spirit as experienced through the vastness of winter, the giddy glory of midsummer night and the tough, solitary individuals who had inhabited this magical abode.

Denmark

The tradition of Danish folk music is very rich and may be considered one of the oldest directions of popular music. Before the beginning of the twentieth century folk music was a much more part of the culture of the average Dane as it was in use in almost all social gatherings like celebrations, farming and time-passing activities as well as in most households. However, as for the folk songs and music mentioned earlier, Denmark still has plenty of living traditions of folk music present in today's Danish society all across the country.

Various musical instruments that go back to thousands of years show that Danes were also into music and this has been confirmed by music archeologists. The first tools include flutes, lures bronze trumpets belonging to the bronze age and other string instruments. In medieval music, it is evident that most of the music was religious especially the Roman Catholic Church though there were some civilian songs and dance music most of them were by the farmers and other ignorant people. Songs for the old pols and other community dances were accompanied by fiddles, pipes and the humble, which is a form of zither.

In the 16th – 18th centuries folk music was listened to with great enthusiasm even though the church did not approve it. Violins and accordions were employed for dance music when there appeared polka and waltz and they spread all over Europe. In the 19th century, more developed Danish composers, for example, J. P. E. Hartmann gradually used more genuine folk songs in their works. It also stimulated people's consciousness in the field of living folk tradition of Denmark which was regained through the Romantic Nationalist movement. Although people like Svend Grundtvig were just laymen, he began collecting songs that he got from the farmers and other simple folks. Publications like books helped in putting folk tunes within the reach of the readers especially those from the urban areas.

More efforts to collect and notate the Danish folk genres were made in the 20th century when the tradition was slowly losing its relevancy to the modernization processes. More than fifty thousand field pieces of the country's nearly extinct folk music were recorded by hearers such as H. Grüner-Hegge, Evald Tang Kristensen and Thorkild Knudsen. As for the specifics of the development of interest to folk music the action that played a significant role was the Danish folk revival of the 70s. Even to date, they practice superstitions, though not original practice, but revived ones that are in Denmark. However, the source has been saving a great deal of information on the folk music of Denmark.

At the same time, Denmark has an individual sound due to the development of special instruments and music genres during the existence of Danish music. They include the fiddle, the accordion, and flutes, as well as the various plucked and bowed zithers. Today the hardingfele or the pear-shaped fiddle can be considered the most typical Danish folk instrument and is used in dance music.

Related instruments include violin or guitar and mandolins tuned in standard or any other tuning.

Other instruments that commonly occur in traditional dance forms include double-reeded instruments including clarinets, accordions, concertinas and harmoniums. The flopfløjte also known as the willow flute is commonly employed in the music of herdmen. Other related pin instruments are the humle plucked zither, mandora, and one of the guitar's relatives such as langeleik. There is also an obvious link between the jouhikko variants and the bowed zithers with the nyckelharpa of Sweden. Bagpipes were introduced in the mid part of the nineteenth century as part of the military bands. The lur, bukkehorn and wooden shepherd's horns are historical forms of signaling horns that are in existence to date.

As far as the styles are concerned, Danish folk is full of dance music due to the historic backgrounds of the people that encompass more of the communal dancing and pleasure grounds. Fiddling jazz has dances such energetic tunes as zithers, accordions, and vocals with many people dancing at once. Some types are based on vocals such as herding and hunting songs, sacred songs, traditional songs and ballads, and occasional solo fiddle songs among others. Another type of singing is choral singing and most of these songs are sung without accompaniments or instruments. The elements of Danish dance music and instruments have also been featured in modern folk-rock/roots music as well.

Several characters played significant roles in the preservation of the folk tradition as well as the growth process of the same in Denmark through the ages. In the Romantic period, they imitated the folk tunes in their compositions as is evident from the music scores of C. E. F Weyse and J. P. E Hartmann. It was also during this period that people like Grüner-Hegge, Svend Grundtvig, Evald Tang Kristensen, and Thorkild Knudsen among others began the process of field recording and transcribing the folk music from such rural centers where it was threatened near extinction.

About that time Livonian also addresses contemporary performers as vital agents who help renewing the Danish folk. The following are some the today's revival groups; Dreamers' Circus, Habadekuk and Rannok should also be mentioned. Other performers are fiddlers, Søren Frank, Harald Haugaard, Kristian Bugge and accordionists Mette Kathrine Jensen. Some musicians also incorporated folk influences in different popular trends; among progressive-rock musicians Secret Oyster and amongst pop musicians Sorten Muld. Other ethnomusicologists, who have researched and recorded Denmark's living folk music are Lisbet Torp and Eva Fock.

Many of the typical Danish folk tunes and songs have titles given by composition authors or places connected with these works. For example, "Lars Kruse's springdance" is a title that was borrowed from the fiddler Lars Kruse who set the melody. The furniture pols are obtainable from a place in Funen which is very famous for cabinet-making. The other category is songs that chronicle the folklore or the historical touchstones for which the music in question was produced. These names reveal the interaction that Denmark has with geography and people and local music.

However, Denmark is a small country, regional folk styles developed within the country based on the area's people's musical tastes and regional cultural strata differences between the provinces. Nevertheless, from region to region, there is also a significant amount of interaction as well as borrowing of ideas. In a general sense, funnel-shaped fiddles are further to the west of the region, specifically in western Jutland, while the members of the violin family are further to the east, in the islands.

As long as anyone can remember, there has deeply been set into the traditions across this area a tradition of Hardanger fiddling styled.

Here and around, area fiddle players create longer more drone-based melodies. They also set more scratchy sounds on the strings, which are relatively open in position. The use of Pols with speed and structure is also practiced in Central Jutland. Traditionally, musical styles Bornholm makes use of the baltic and Scotland styles much more bagpipe bowed lyre, which forms an integral part. Very good folklore cultures can be found in Lolland and Falster, which to a large extent are influenced by Sweden because both kingdoms passed into Swedish hands at the end of the 18th century.

A critical review of the literature shows diverse means of expressing dance and musical tuning, and that concerning the fiddle music of Funen. The strong development of rhythmic harmonics is marked by intervals of fourths, and the striking way dual stops are employed, to underline the melody. The folk here have a rich tradition full of historical customs and local color, which has set it quite apart from the Nordic music styles. Yet Fiddle, Accordion, and Zither play their part with Love songs and Folk-dances even today. It is, in truth, only today that Denmark thus preserves its musical Tradition by putting these instruments in its museums; but the prosperity of such collections is owing to the existence of an appreciative audience. Besides, it has been proved that folk music has existed as an art form for many centuries.

Norway

Norwegian folk music faced its roots back in the Middle Ages. During the Medieval period, people of Scandinavian cultures loved music and drama, especially minstrels who performed songs and dances and the people also liked listening to ballads. The genes of some of the older dance tunes and ballads that circulated among the populations were transmitted orally, particularly in the more remote areas. The most famous one is "Draumkvedet" which is a ballad tragic story of Olav Åsteson while it is believed to have originated in the 14th century. It has been transmitted orally for generations and remains to make the listeners get a chill down their spine.

Norwegian folk also centered on the tradition of seafaring as the country is among the most seafaring ones. Sailing along the coast they promoted music and received impressions from other cultures among them. They also sang stories while in fishing or whaling boats and they did it in the form of songs. There are heard metrical allusions to rowing, hoisting the sails, chopping, and sawing in the folk songs of the Norwegians. The Viking Age was also significant from the cultural point of view and there are still songs sung by today's folk singers, stories of Vikings and myths.

The new Christian religion got into Norway in the early millennium and the medieval church was chiefly concerned with the development of vocal and chorale. The only songs that have an even more archaic background as they sang many songs are those that directly evoked biblical psalms or such happy situations as Christmas or Midsummer. Even some of the religious folk songs too have their pagan influences but were slowly changed to fit the new religion. The music of the Norwegian also has melancholic aspects consisting of slow tempo and minor piano keys appropriate for long winters. Other large categories are funeral music and songs that are dedicated to death.

Outside court and church, Norwegian farmers and laborers developed their music based on folkish community experiences passed from one generation to another. By far the majority of the Norwegian folk stems from dance music or is situational and specifically connected to the act of telling a certain story and certain life situations.

Norwegian folk music for the most part is string-based music instruments. Thus, we find that except for the Hardanger fiddle, flat fiddle, regular violin, 12–string guitar and the langeleik, the instruments have different tonal qualities. Wind instruments like the bukkehorn (goat horn), lur (hollowed horn) and munnharpe (mouth harp) lack refinement hence providing the music with a raw feel.

There are some of the oldest dances which include the Halling and springar that are performed in events conducted in the rural valleys and use the fiddle and guitar in their dance. The Swibel/ Deutsch and the Pols also turned into the other country dance forms that which were identified to be performed in the country. Some can be even long extended story songs to shortest lyrical songs about love with nature and daily feels. Originally, they were chanted without instruments and were played by fiddlers alone without other musical instruments.

Norway has a vast number of vocal traditions that go from lone fjords and even valleys in the whole country. Cries, ditties and chanting without words that imitate the actual real-life phenomena are incorporated by the ancients in the songs. Certain forms of singing which include, but are not limited to, kulning or herding calls, laling or lelloing vocal expressions, are made possible by the resonance of voices within the spaces. The use of folk choir also preserves the motifs of the Middle Ages while the doubled vocals sound also does the same.

Herding songs that include ex. Kulokker imitates the bell sound to guide cattle. Horn signals, alarms, whistling signals DIRECTION direction are used to convey messages for a considerably long distance. The use of Jtering is to inform that the show is over and it is time to go home while in their specific calls, animals are given names. The lokk is a special kind of grazing song that is sung to animals. The latter include midsummer, hunting, Christmas, and wedding songs.

The foremost of the Norwegian composers was Edvard Grieg who contributed a great deal in collating and notating the Norwegian folk songs. Grieg borrowed from his pieces for solo piano and produced the following folk-based themes of his Peer Gynt Suite. He introduced people in the various parts of the globe with Norway folk tunes through his music.

Myllarguten (1801 – 1872) is reckoned to have brought the Hardanger to even purer, more artistic styles. The active influence of composers across Scandinavia tells a clear story of revival during the 19th century. He was born in a small village in Telemark but was celebrated all over Norway as the "King of fiddlers", and who traveled around the country with concerts and competitions. To his peers like Halling-Knut and Lars Fykerud he took over these impressive repertoires.

As one of the most important popularisers of the old Norwegian song heritage, Kirsten Bråten Berg has contributed to both, preserving and further development of the old song tradition. She grows from a Telemark farming family and she uses regional accents and her dances which are not common even in the larger general vales, let alone the world. As the director of the National Folk Music and Dance Society, Berg loves to hand down folk arts from one generation to another.

Thus, Norway also has an established system of folk musicians and dancers and has the official National Association of Folk Music and Folk Dancers. Such societies are useful in transmitting information from one generation to the other, archiving important records, planning on festivals, concerts and education among others. Amid other impressive collections of 19th-century tunes collected by Ludvig Mathias Lindeman, many songs that otherwise would have been lost to history were saved. They are also still quoted and performed by scholars and performers even to the present generation.

Therefore, it is quite pertinent to posit, that the folk elements have had a direct imprint on modern music in Norway. Freestyle jazz which features America's film-score pioneer Jan Garbarek adopts folksong to some of its flagship records. Modern musicians, like Susanne Sundfør, Aurora or Kings of Convenience, despite their indie-pop style songs, carry ancient ballad feelings of Norwegian lands. Stars still reflect the folk of Norway's well; genres remain progressive.

Nor can it be judged as invalid because of the closeness to modern Norwegian national music identity, nor can it be argued that the folk music of Norway is little connected to the Norway of reality because folk music is the reality for Norway. On one hand, it is a connection of the country to the history or the past while on the other it is an object the meaning of which is evolving or opening the theme of Norwegian identity. The spirit of a culture as long as it is passed to the next generations Norwegian one-of-a-kind music will always have an essential place in the Norwegian people and contemporary music soundscapes.

Sweden

What about Swedish folk music? Well, Swedish folk music's history begins way before the current generation and as such, it is a very active folk music tradition. Scandinavian people had very old folk vocal and instrumental music and the traditional songs at the early stage consisted of herding calls, ballads and legends, has were taught and handed down from one generation to another. These depicted the existence, work, ethics and stories, which are the essentials of agrarian Nordic culture. It also revealed that early folk instrumentation with what materials were within reach was also introduced, they include the willow flute, cattle horn and the rather crude fiddles made of mere wood.

Some of the first songs include the kulning that were an early type of herding call; the ballads (visas) that recite folk stories and myths of love or death, and heroes and legends that depict trolls or witches. Small folk dances with fast, lively stepping also were included and were usually played with a fiddle or an accordion. It was raw, and regional and differed from farm, to forest, to seashore, and from one part of the Nordic countries to another.

Sweden also underwent the Agricultural Revolution and Industrialization in the 19th century since people of different communities started communicating as a result of infrastructure accommodation. Most folk music repertories gained increased regional and social stratification in such situations as public or communal dances or private or formal occasions such as weddings. New customs also arose as to how certain festivals are celebrated either annually.

Over time the urban bourgeoisie began to be interested in acquiring specimens of folk music for study since they viewed country music as their culture. This paved way for preservation as industrialization was singled out to have wiped out tradition that is old world village culture. Some of these collectors were Nils Andersson, Gunnar Wennerberg and Johan Halvorsen who wrote down the songs. Moreover, folk musicians can be listed among public appreciation such as fiddlers Byss-Calle and Hjort Anders Olsson whose tunes are still played today.

The Swedish composers, scholars, and performers in the late 19th-century planning to develop national folk music; they chose those musical practices that reflected the 'Swedish' spirit selectively and thereby constructing what is known as today's Swedish folk music for patriotism while eradicating the diversifying rural music traditions.

Some of the leaders of the Swedish folkmusik movement included artist Carl Larsson who was depictively and idealistically painting Swedish country life; and fiddler Johan Helmrich Roman who was studying the repertoires. Other characters were musician Wilhelm Peterson Berger, who wrote sentimental piano music inspired by folk songs of Sweden, and the painter Anders Zorn, who vigorously advanced the cause of the two-tone Dala horse, traditionally painted red color of the falu region of Sweden.

This cultural engineering for common folk music began preservation as early as the establishment of the first 'Nordiska Museet' in the year 1873 and listing of the tunes. It also introduces renewed interest to other instruments like the nyckelharpa, or the keyed fiddle unique to Sweden. Yet, as Savilaakso has demonstrated, the folk music movement which aimed at defining some songs and melodies as 'proper' and 'true' Swedish, had omitted Sami joiks. Nevertheless, Orkester was able to set up basic characteristics of Swedish folk music on the level of national awareness.

As romanticized images of rural folk life were gradually challenged by the advance of the modernization process folksongs experienced more mini-renaissances. Fiddlers' teams or spelmanslag were formed in Sweden to revive the declining fiddle and dancing traditions of their country. On that, some performers continued what some folks do in the future by following international pop music.

Some revival musicians were; fiddler Jon-Erik Hall who spent much time in the study and revival of almost lost Swedish pieces. Other bands that also began the process in the 80s composed an array of "group music" for groups, which intervened in American Jazz/Rock with Nordic folk. Next to folk songs, elements from the folklore were carried by emigrants, dances like the Swedish schottis.

Gaelic folk music of Sweden had been transformed since the late 1900s from the rural music that had been revived but also was evolving. It included everyone from the cult ethnic band Hedningarna to singers like Sofia Karlsson whose music also incorporated jazz/pop. Swedish fiddles, horns and strings appeared in musical panorama and became part of different styles. To this very day, Swedish folk is in a continuous process of becoming anew, with tradition being the force that propels the move into the future in a process of re-creation.

Swedish folk music also entails the use of several instruments some of which developed in northern Europe before any of the other known instruments. Key instruments include:

Fiddle (Fel or Fiol): The most known Swedish folk musical instrument is a vibraphone which looks like a pear, the size of the violin and it is strung. One of the variants is the flat-bridged fiddle of Dalarna.

Nyckelharpa: A bowed lyre as specific to Sweden with keys on the strings. It is indispensable in folk tradition: to passed on and used in signaling messages that are imperative, its sound is authoritative and musical.

Willow Flute (Sälgflöjt): Stone age artifact of the aerophonic flutes of the flute type hand made from willow branches. Contributes to a light and otherworldly feel of the tone.

Lur: It is an antique curved brass horn going by the name of Viking Age horn that was used for herding animals or calling them from a long distance. Produces loud, trumpet-like tones.

Cattle Horn (Bukkehorn): An instrument used in shepherds' activities as a tool for driving the stock which was created from cow horns. Creates low buzzing tones.

Accordion/ Harmonium: The free-reed aerophones have their origin in continental Europe has been classified to be relevant for Nordic dances.

Jews Harp (Munnharpe): A small metallic cylindrical instrument that is attached on the palms and struck against one another and then held by the lips to produce musical notes. Common in folk repertoires.

Stringed Instruments: Over time, folk musicians changed several stringed instruments like lutes, zithers, and guitars for accompanimental chord.

Other usual body instruments have also been played in Swedish folk music, for example, the tuned antler bones which were clicked in a musical beat. Some of the items that I noticed that were used in the play of the music included rolling pins and spoons that were used to play several dance tunes.

Swedish folk music can be defined as a complex of regional songs and dances as well as vocal practices. These include:

Ballads (Visas): A traditional song or ballad is a type of song that recants an old story, a legend, a fairy tale, a tragedy or an epic. Has been recorded for instance in its cappella form and for voices and percussion instruments only.

Herding calls (Kulning): Natural methods of communication used by the herders to call for their cattle that give a produce similar to that of yodeling.

Waulking songs (Vallning): Songs that were performed in parallel tunes whilst threshing grain or beating cloth. Feature strong vocal harmonization.

Dance styles: People-friendly and called rhythmic tunes which are very close to various kinds of folk and country dances. Among the forms familiar to the participant, names of the lively Swedish Polska 2/4 or 3/4, schottis, mazurka, waltz, and menuett can be mentioned.

Work and celebratory songs: Singing of songs that narrate events of sowing, reaping, hoeing or singing at harvest time and Midsummer.

Joik: One of the oldest forms of Sámi singing; the rhetoric of which is an improvised verse set to an improvised tune and is a story or an image.

The positive expressions are found in songs with percussion, herding calls and joyful tunes and the ballad and the pastoral songs and chants have lyrical music. It is pertinent to observe that the core of the Swedish folk vocals is based on high-pitched, bright source voices that are clearly protruded forward.

Swedish folk music encompasses distinct regional styles, instruments and dances reflecting local geography and culture: Swedish folk Music has different areas and different styles, and local instruments and dances related to the style of living:

Northern (Norrland): The old and archaic forms of vocal music that embrace horn calls including the kulning herding call. Willow flute traditions. Forest/pastoral themes.

Central (Svealand): As a result, Nyckelharpa traditions were concentrated on the Uppland. Pretty fiddle and dance music such as the Swedish Polska. Storytelling ballads.

Southern (Götaland): A few of them can be attributed to European / Germanic roots while the rest are rooted as basic elements. Popular tunes for accordion formation to include schottis and polka. Ancient lur horns were used.

Indigenous Sámi (Lapland): Indigenous Arctic people practiced voice singing inclusive of the people who were occupied with the rearing of reindeer. Throat singing elements.

Dalarna (Falun-Dala): The very core of archetypal representations of the Swedes and the Sweden. Bright two-color red Dala horse signature. Ornamented fiddle for instance is an exciting play of staccato melodies especially in music that is related to dance music for instance slängpolska.

West Coast & Lake Regions: Other local forms include uppåtäfsa which are variants of Danish/Norwegian pols such as Valår, Vårväder, Godnatt for jultomten and Midsommarmarknad. Songs that relate to workplaces and in particular those sung by fishermen and seamen.

Swedish-Speaking Regions of Finland: Musical related and closely related genres in the neighborhood of the Gulf of Bothnia – for example, effecting such as Österbotten fiddle/accordion dance music.

These are just a few – folk music remains highly differentiated by the geographical origin, and grouping even though efforts were made in the nineteenth century to centralize folk music. It is also evident that the growth of urban centres as well as trade and migration and interaction across cultures also played a leading role in its evolution within the region.

The country has produced some of the greatest folk artists and it also possesses a very strong musical ethos. A few seminal icons who crucially shaped Swedish folk are highlighted below by era: Some of the most influential pioneers who significantly influenced the development of Sweden folk music are described below in chronological order:

Byss-Calle (1600s-1700s): A fiddler from the Swedish area of Dalarna who throughout has numerous successful tunes that are still played to this day. His most successful piece of work is still what is referred to as the "Devil's Polska".

Hjort Anders Olsson (1800s): One of the most famous fiddlers from Uppland who is believed to have written more than 500 tunes. Had a great influence on the development of Swedish nyckelharpa culture.

Wilhelm Peterson-Berger (1867-1942): a composer who wrote romantic piano solos that referred to Swedish folk tunes including the "Frösö Flower." Attempted to add more harmonies to the particular folk tunes.

Jenny Lind (1820-1887): Singing and touring other countries for her performances, a famous opera singer of Sweden who made the Swedish folksongs famous was, referred to as the Swedish Nightingale.

Karin Ingmarsdotter (1869 - 1961): Swedish keyed fiddle or nyckelharpa master and there are more than twelve thousand compositions credited to him. Unmissable tradition maintainer for more than half a century.

Emil Smith-Säfström (1868-1926): Collected and recorded over 20 thousand dallies that were characteristic of Sweden to preserve them from the process of oblivion because of the forces of modernization.

Nils Andersson (1821-1880): A traditional ethnographic folk music collector, who recorded many traditional vocals and instruments music pieces and nowadays they can be published in the Music Museum of Stockholm.

J. H Roman (1826-1888): Both accompanied and committed fiddling tunes as well as supported ideals of preserving and eradicating Swedish folk customs. Composed new fiddle tunes that seemed to be a continuation of the new folk archetypes.

Jon-Erik Hall (1938-2014): Folk singer, whose main interest in the joyful pastime was to gather and spread various unknown to many Swedish fiddling/fiddle traditions. You could find out that you have restored digital worn-out antiquities that had been written in manuscripts of the older days for modern use.

Groupa (the mid-1900s): The initiators of the new wave of Swedish "group music," which translates elements of American pop/rock trends and motives of Swedish folklore. Inspired later folk fusions.

Sofia Karlsson (1975-present): Folk-pop artist from Sweden who is also a contemporary artist with folk and pop jazz, she offers new jazz for folk songs as an interpreted artist.

Swedish folk music encompasses a mosaic of rituals and seasonal customs including The Swedish folk music contains a spectrum of rituals and seasonal entertainment which are:

St Lucy's Day Celebrations (St Lucia): Midwinter pagan rituals of the solstice, Yule, amorphous white-robed singing ceremonies that this Lucia means – the 'light' in the darkest hours.

Maypole Dances (Majstång): Religious ceremonies linked to the birth of spring to epitomize the return of nature by way of happy-bearing dancers in white garments and the fasteners in ribbons on the tall pole. Music accompanies.

Midsummer Festivities: HAPPY MIDSUMMER with food and drinks and fun with flower crown maypoles all over mid-June in Sweden.

Life Passage Rituals: As a part of the folk music that is considered to be indispensable parts of the eternal Nordic ceremonies of birth, marriage, and death.

Wakes (Likvaka): Prayers or hymn-like songs said around the time of death or for the dead, for instance, hymns that were sung all through the night.

Herding Signals (Kulning): The Nordic herders used Stone Age technology of communication in signaling or rallying their cattle. Yodeling-like vocals give the alert on the ground while it is eerie.

Hunting Calls: Silver trumpets of the Viking epoch from Nordic hunting and vocal imitative calls in the form of shouts.

These are only a few examples of the most important Swedish folk traditions – seasonal ceremonies, agricultural celebrations, and religious practices have always involved singing throughout the territory. Some persisted through the ages while others wanted but all changed with time and space.

Swedish folk regained interest during the mid-late twentieth century as more and more attempt was made to capture the rural lifestyles and music associated with the eve of tradition. It encouraged the renewed value of traditions once nearly extinct, as old players seeking repatriation found endangered cultural songs for modern revival.

Organization efforts also emerged in the vein of conservation such as Svenska Folkdansringen (Swedish Folk Dance Association) The media in the form of folk music magazines, festivals, competitions, and radio programs provided fresh circulation.

A wealth of hidden historical material thus received new light – from the 13th-century ballad "Herr Peder och Herr Mogens" revived by 1970s researcher Gunnar Granberg to archaic medieval herding calls restored by Kulning researcher Susanne Rosenberg's work. Revival musicians also reignited interest by recording new works based on old pieces such as when nyckelharpist Eric Sahlstrom of Swedish-American origin recorded new compositions to traditional historical pieces.

In a way, Swedish folk also actively reimagined themselves through cultural appropriation - importing outside stimuli while recalibrating them for future, new artistic needs.

This was often achieved through the cross-genre collaborations, such as the Frifot band from Sweden where folk singers were accompanied by jazz trio. Some incorporated Nordic folk elements within rock music, for example, Swedish fiddler in progressive folk band Garmarna in Gesaelig; of the 1990s or pop rock ballad "Vandraren" (Wanderer) by the Finnish band Nordman. Some artists also took Swedish folk instruments to a completely different territory, for example, percussionist Staffan Astner playing jazz improvisations on willow flute.

Besides such hybrids, there are such types that genres imported which had incorporated into Swedish folk custom over time imitatively, adaptively, and assimilatively. For instance, accordions which were earlier assimilated as extraneous components are now inseparable components of Scandinavian dance music and are now regarded as being part of 'folk' instruments of the region. Polka and waltz forms, however, were incorporated so deeply with the indigenous Swedish dances that completely new dances which as svensk vals (Swedish waltz).

As with migrational transplants of cultures, Swedish folk have been moved and/or dealing with people of other tongues through the Nordic communities throughout various countries – during famines or otherwise as with Mid-1800 emigration. They thus took tradition to the new locations they moved to for example how Norwegian immigration brought in concepts like the enduring Spelmanslag otherwise referred to as the "fiddlers club" model to the United States.

Overseas groups, however, continued the Swedes' folk relation for generations. Proof of this long cultural imprint lies in the Nordic festivals embracing the present-day innovations including Minnesota's Skärvången Fiddle Camp, where the youths learning the Swedish tunes, dance, and artistry are in other nations. Swedish Americans also remained ongoing and they were bringing in more teachers and performers as far as folk scene programming in twin cities is concerned.

Besides diasporas, still, other aficionados of historical or authentic cultural tradition throughout the world have also assimilated Sweden's folk revival, whether as players of an instrument as complicated in construction and with as uncertain lineage as the nyckelharpa or as performers of dances as un-Swedish as the Engelska Quadrille. Swedish folk is therefore alive and well; people from all corners of the globe can participate in the online lessons and collaborations; for instance, there are Japanese people in the Folk You band and Nyckelharpa Orchestra has members from different continents. Therefore, the characters' far-sounding melodies turn into accented – the mutual exchange between the home country and the customs of emigrants.

As for the future of Swedish folk music, it will most likely also evolve in a quite active manner as the musicians themselves attempt to find out how this received tradition can be further developed while trying something new at the same time. For this reason, further discourses about such conceptions as 'authenticity' will proceed - as well as discourses about balancing preserving some of these works to some extent or extent of enabling the culture to transform.

However, if its continued narrative is anything, Swedish folk music is flexible and viable – capable of incorporating new instruments, half-breed singers and players, or teenagers who have learned 'folk' anew but are not stagnant. The fundamental Opera of local epistemologies thus persists as the constant in this emergent re-coding of rituals, and the celebratory ethic.

As it is clear from the discussion under consideration, Swedish folk music has entered quite a long journey from the context of rural settings and though it has been interrupted due to advancement in technology, it has been supported through tradition bearers. As revivalists continue to maintain and innovators take folk forms into the future – the next goes one step further towards more.

Thus, Swedish folk music is full of different regional characteristics, traditional practices and local specificity about the identity of the North. It mixes the motifs from folk ballads and stories, pastourelle elements; rurality, additional application of fiddles, nyckelharpas, willow flutes, and folk dances. Swedish folk is a concept of history and also of caretakers and creators, where Swedish reclaim and create themselves – invoking hereditary days that are far from dead and alive in the sound of today through fresh blood.

Finland

Finns have always been curious about folk music even if this type of music has developed in Finland for centuries. It is a type of folk music, which had its roots in non-Christian traditions and customs, shepherds' signals as well as poetry and has evolved itself to be a part of the Finnish people. With time even specialization came into foray – mighty vocal techniques – extraordinary Finnish instruments- that began to define & set apart Finnish folk music. In as much as the genre was already on its decline by the twentieth century, there are still works from the Finnish folk artists and revival movements.

Today, even in the most popular genres, one can still trace relations to Finnish folk music.

The Finnish region has a musical history since the time of remote forests and some small villages in the region that are part of Nordic countries. Folk music has served purposes for centuries for communication and organization of tasks like herding calls when one has to herd cattle or goats, rowing work songs— songs that are recited while rowing in boats, rhyming spells for everyday chores before it was turned into an art and became the identity of culture as is known today. Finnish folk music stems from three primary sources: Finnish folk music can be derived from three different fountains.

Ancient Shamanistic Practices: It has been claimed to have been practiced since prehistoric man as well as the poets, ritual drumming and chanting by the shamans who populated the area of today's Finland. These singing traditions were a chance to appeal to the animal spirits for good hunting and thereby secured the part of the rhythmic vocality in Finnish music.

Kalevala Poetry: The Finnish poems and folklore collected in the middle of the nineteenth century having a name, Kalevala has evoked significant effects on the themes and singing style of Finnish folk music with rhythmic alliteration. They used to say that the major part of the history, myths, and legends is preserved in the Kalevala poems which were later used as the basis for the further folk songs and ballads in final. In this way, the poem established the power of the story in the Finnish oral tradition in Finnish folklore.

Herding and Work Songs: The stems of the subjects are in agricultural areas, and historical popular music includes songs in the fields. In this regard, the herders found a way of educating the animals by singing to them which was referred to as kulning. Among different types of singing (schöne singen) of the Finnish folk, the later ornate was accompanied by the callings of kulning – shrill, echoing yodels. Round dance shouts were also identified on the large trading vessels. They demonstrate that these working chants have shifted into a genuine song and dance format over sections of timespan.

Over the centuries, Finnish folk music culture coalesced around five major regional styles named after the lands and people that produced them: Karelian, Ingrian, Savonian and Pelimanni and Kaustinen fiddle is the generic name for most contemporary instrumental folk music of the peoples inhabiting Finland and neighboring countries. Each regional style, however, had specific features: the trochaic rhythm of kaustinen tunes, the burial march of Russian-accompanied karelian runs, and so on – at the same time, all of it originated from the shamanistic, collective body of melodic cliches. The music of the Finnish people was becoming part of the nationality over the nineteenth and at the beginning of the twentieth century. Nonetheless, industrialization and the change of culture in Finland paved the way for the decrease in appreciation of the genre until the 1900s were the revival movement gave value and appreciation to the novelty of the distinctive Scandinavian style.

Many people are familiar with this type of music in Finland and this type of music comes with a sad melody and this is attributed to the type of instruments that are used with it. The evolution of Finnish folk music instruments has only slightly changed, and what was produced hundreds of years ago is not that much dissimilar to what was produced in the late 20th century – strings, woodwind instruments, and basic percussion instruments above all. Key instruments and related vocal techniques include:

Kantele: The national instrument of Finland is the kantele however it is a lap harp made with metal strings and possessing a wooden sound box whose base is carved from a single piece of wood. Being a constant beating rhythm to most folk tunes the kantele is part of most Finnish folk groups and provides heavenly accompaniment to many folk songs. With more intensity, fast plucking provides lively dance tunes while light and slow bowing complements the singers' mournful, sad tunes.

Fiddle: The other key instrument in Finnish folk music, rendered for both tunes and songs was one of the most suitable fiddles, the simple one. The centuries saw periods forming regional styles of folk fiddling; the bouncy syncopated rhythmic combined to be recognized as the Kaustinen stile, the faster and minor key playing associated with the Pelimanni stile.

Woodwinds: Reed aerophones inclusive of the clarinet, accordion, flute and harmonium are used in folk-based bands. In some regions such as Russian Karelia, woodwinds transmit the melody in the Slavic-influenced hail. In some areas, bagpipes and hurdy-gurdies also appeared to provide a more solemn, according to the timbre, bass tone or drone.

Resonant Singing: That is why vocals reign most of the time in Finnish folk music regardless of whether it is an epic, poetry or dance. Kulning is performed, intentionally by many singers to further amplify the sound making it nearly yodel-like to mimic the echo of the calls across the forests and fields of Finland before today's technology was in use. Kulning is the basis for how we give a certain timbre to Finnish folk music. Incorporation of manipulate trills and short slides between the high head voice and low chest voice helps in resonance thus supporting the dramatic, ornate vocals that are expected in this particular form of singing. Another type of added-on note is also found in sociable folk songs and dance tunes most especially rowing songs.

Besides the classification and the use of the instruments and singing styles, another criterion that separated Finnish folk music from other traditional folk was language and lyrics. It is for this reason that even though a significant number of the Finland country folk still speak the foreign language fluently especially English, the majority still prefer to speak their national languages. Of the songs and the ballads, some are of Kalevala origin and are made to sound archaic and magical. Today singers still find inspiration in the Karelian poetic that inspired most of the folk music over two hundred years back. The following are some of these traditions which have not been changed in the genre even up to the present generation.

Industrialization was threatening the continuation of Indigenous culture and performing arts in the nineteenth and earlier twentieth centuries, but resilient artists and restart movements kept the beat of Finnish folk music for decades. With the assistance of the researchers who gathered Karelian poems in the 19th century, when rock groups in the 1970s wanted to use components of both modern and folk rock, the genre developed further with the aid of those who did not the old Finnish traditions to vanish completely. The most critical contributors to the enduring longevity of Finnish folk music include: Experimentation, along with other concerns as specified in the following sub-sections are the most significant elements that have kept Finnish folk music alive and relevant for the longest time:

Elias Lönnrot: The collecting of oral Karelian folklore epics such as by Elias Lönnrot in the first half of the 19-century that led to the compilation of the first volume of the Kalevala in 1835 is perhaps one of the single most significant factors that helped the country develop a strong folk musical tradition. When the Epic entered the culture, the subjects, tales and myths portrayed in the verses gave several later folk singers, musicians and dancers the impetus to continue the art associated with the stories of The Kalevala.

Old-Time Folk Bands: Minstrels in small family bands moving from one village to the other entertaining the public by singing and acting out folk songs and short comedies ensured that folk music was alive in the late 19th and early 20th centuries. These usually amateurish groups were mainly located in northern Savonia and performed both regional folk instruments ranging from fiddles to Hebrew lyres. Some of these groups included the Järvelä Family Band, a band that has been performing for over sixty years and the Kontran Band, a band which had multi-generational performers and Jewish klezmer influences to their folk tones giving different tonal colours.

1960s Folk Revival: Young Finns discovered folk music in the 1960s and the folk scene was kicking in Helsinki and more popular bands, such as Cumulus were formed using old influences. As with many revival groups, they also introduced new inventions that blended Finnish folk songs and ballads with Rock instruments and political protest lyrics. This folk revival in the context of the sixties awakened the interest of the entire nation in almost forgotten rural traditions which subsequently led to the launch of festivals, radio programs, competitions and archives dedicated to the Finnish folk arts. Further preservation efforts are derived from this era.

Värttinä: No band can be regarded as the successful synthesis of Finnish folk influences with global tendencies in music more successfully than Värttinä. meaning "spindle" in Finnish, Värttinä was formed in 1983 to fuse the traditional singing and the Karelian kantele tradition with the modern voice and international instruments ranging from strings to synthesizers. They introduced the Finnish folk to the international stage with their initial album Seleniko which received appreciation across borders followed by 6 more albums and 3 Grammy nominations in the next two decades. Their sound is still authentic folk yet it is constantly exploring new frontiers of what Finnish music can be when played in a plugged-in manner.

The Kaustinen Folk Music Festival: Building on the folk revival of the 1960s, local officials of the small town of Kaustinen in central Finland founded an annual folk music festival in 1968 to promote national and regional performers as the genre continued to gain popularity. It is the largest Nordic folk festival of its kind with more than 30,000 fans and 500 musicians attending the event every July. The festival includes instrumental and song and dances, folk, orchestral, vocal, and jam sessions, and an International Folk Music Film Festival. This much-loved summer event is still raising awareness of contemporary folk artists from Finland even today, more than half a century on.

The simple and sad notes of today's Finnish folk music, which are based on pentatonic and modal scales, penetrated beyond the distant Lapland and forest countryside to affect the world music in one or another way during the century. It gave ideas to the classical music composers, enriched political song-writing movements and can be heard as a background for popular music that touches the complex folk base of the Finish music of the contemporary period.

Jean Sibelius: Finnish most famous classical composer Jean Sibelius received lifetime honor and recognition for his grandiose nationalist tone poems such as Finlandia and 'The Karelia Suite' that painted the enigmatic Finnish geographical terrain in pitch and timbre. However, the basis for his symphonic themes was found in the Karelian folk songs and songs, words and myths that he heard in the peasant settlements of Karelia where he used to go. The modal colour or timbre of

Finnish folksongs and ballads offered Sibelius the themes for his imperialistic orchestrations.

American Folk & Protest Music: During the period of folk music craze in the United States around the early 1960s, many singers including Peter, Paul and Mary resorted to Finnish folk songs for new material in non-English language as the changing world demanded more political songs. Their cover of "Leaving on a Jet Plane", originally composed in 1962 by Pirkka-Pekka Petelius from Finland as "Käymme Yhdessä Läpi" brought weepy Finnish ballad sounds to American radio waves and some used Finnish folk in protest songs against war and injustice.

Metal and Rock Fusions: The motives and themes of the folk music of the Scandinavian countries are incorporated by many extreme metal bands from Northern Europe into the images that depict certain moods and persons for numerous and complex and dark-sounding compositions. In the case of Finnish bands like for example; Amorphis, Korpiklaani, and Ensiferum, the national folk riffs from an instrument like kantele or jouhikko fiddle along with folk singing techniques helped in popularising a subgenre of folk metal. This goes to show that Finland is still capable of raising musicians that are popular among the youth.

Finns also employ their folk music in this process of change starting from the shamanistic phase to the World tours but with basically Finnish identity and regional traits. Although the development of various phenomena and technologies threatened the extinction of this genre, enthusiasts of the music and true fans did not want to see the old traditions be eradicated. Not surrendering to the situation, innovative musicians discovered a way to mix the old and the new, to take Finnish folk into the future - so that the ghost melodies of kanteles, herders' whistles and notes, and sad songs could resonate for years. Thus, it might be said that the true, genuine Finnish folk are not only lost somewhere beyond the reach of this or any other generation but have been reduced to a set of layers in the cultural memory of the people, which may periodically resurface in the popular music of the present day, bearing the timeless imprint of the country's countryside.

Iceland

It might be argued that Icelandic folk music has unique features in terms of its picking pattern, the used instruments as well as its historical incorporation of the novelties and the interaction of the nation with the geographical environment.

The following are features that define Icelandic folk music and differentiate it from other forms of music in the world. The geographical isolation of the country and its predominantly rather less populated rural areas forced a unified kind of music that appears to be intrinsically linked to the country's beauty.

The superior part of Icelandic folk music as compared to most Western music is that they are based more on the pentatonic scales, which indicates that they have five notes per octave rather than seven. Correspondingly, the elements mentioned above are integrated to build up a modal sound that is barbarous and prehistoric to conform to the geographical features of Iceland. The pentatonic scale and the songs that use as a base sound the first tone corresponds to the vast desolated interior of Iceland.

Often, in the case of Icelandic folk rhythms, the beats tend to be very complex and irregular as compared to the most common 4/4 time of pop songs. These asynchronous rhythms refer to the natural rhythms — glaciers, lava flows and the sea of the country, Iceland. In such cases, singing challenges in the form of irregularities are utilized by folk singers, for instance by converting such rhythmical tasks into a driving force.

Appropriate even to early Icelandic farmers, who sang to their cattle across valley pastures, the call-and-response technique is not merely American. Because of this, one of the singers would start singing a note and the other singers would sing it back across the distance, and be able to hear the note bouncing off the mountains. The hus (farmstead) songs are still performed today and, in these songs, call and response vocals are still as evident.

For most of its history, interaction with other cultures was sparse which caused Iceland to become a pool of narrative Gæsrcatal. They recited battle exploits of heroes, recounted folk stories, and reinforced myths that belonged to the previous generations of the people. This tradition is followed by modern artists who recite the poetry set to music and narrate modern-day Icelandic stories.

It is for this reason that the musical instruments commonly used in the folk music of Iceland modified the timbre to match the physical features of the country. An example is the Tshikona and Tshikona which are traditional designs that are normally used in today's functions.

The langspil is one of the oldest Icelandic instruments and is typical of a long box zither that has a one-course string of the melodic type and up to seven other strings which are sympathetic strings. It is bowed swiftly beneath the melody string, giving a harsh and prompt tone resembling Iceland's passion. The langspil is generally played in epic recitative in telling of folk stories and other historical instances.

As we have seen in other Nordic countries, the fiddle is one of the most commonly used instruments in Icelandic folk music. This is perhaps the main reason why the gentle, pure tones of the violin complement the resonant nature of the langspil. The instrument to be mentioned, that is fiddle, is played to generate happy tunes during pleasant moments in life including festivals, weddings or any social activity. In the Icelandic fiddling some of the aspects of the old Norwegian hardingfele tradition are still present.

This plucked dulcimer which arrived in Iceland by the year 1000 has a chordal rhythm accompaniment to the voices. Its ringing is as clear as the beautiful sequences of the northern lights moving in the sky of Iceland. The sound of the psaltery smooths and brings the change in the environment which is rather depressive due to the vastness of the area and absence of people.

Whereas in other cultures the pulse of society, be it village or nation, is exhibited through drums and other idiophones, Iceland's music is supplanted with the pulse of its geography. Thus, the beat and timing of the horse's gallop, sea waves, water flowing from the snow, glaciers splitting, and human voices echoing the walls of the fjords. The geology of the island was very active which meant there were materials available for the drums – lava and for the pipe organs – steam vents.

The use of musical instruments in the past can hardly be said to have been copious but even if this was the case, perhaps the most crucial of all instruments in the music of Iceland is the voice. Soprano and alto of various polyphonic voices are admired in grandiosity and hoarse on the treeless planes with power and richness. In this method, singing is done by the singers, and the audience echoes in return singing a song the same as the singers. Thus, it is entertaining to work with words during long winters that are so typical for the country. The pitch meter and the local pronunciation have been distinguishing features in the spoken language of Iceland throughout history.

The isolation of Iceland for several centuries gradually led to the musical upbringing among the people for the consolidation of the people's unity and as a way of passing information across different districts of the country. This was up until the transportation links opened up and 'outside' influences started introducing themselves into the Southern pride.

The first Scandinavians who came here introduced their Old Norse music which was historical in origin being associated with the Germanic tribes. Skalds recite lyrical compositions or sagas regarding warriors and their lineage. The following forms of daily life music were also sung while working; Farm labor songs, and chants for Viking ships going across the North Atlantic. It may have been the case that they sang as they went about their work or chored like weaving baskets, cooking or nursing babies.

Together with plainsong and psalms, purchased in the course of Christianization, pagan music was complemented at the turn of the millennium around the year 1000 CE. The chants and songs of people in the early times were in Old Norse and the Christian legends about Iceland when people could not accept the pagan belief anymore. In the age of Settlement, the songs that were in circulation were sad tunes that depicted the hardships of living in a hard environment.

By that time, Iceland began to become more involved with Scandinavia and the British Isles which in its turn had enriched the musical composition of the Icelanders. They did this to make the langspil's sound suitable for telling legendary stories. It was maintained also by additional dance music from European courts, where tweed fiddles and harps were used in dancing at the festivals. Most of the European dancer's dance in pairs while the Icelanders opted for lines or sets, more suitable for narrow spaces, and non-numbers divisible by two in the countryside.

This period also had collectors such as saemundur Froði who collected songs with their manuscripts and hymn and religious songs which transformed the Icelandic from a pagan to a Christian nation. Melodies themselves remained only as oral traditions that were handed down from one generation to the next.

Somewhere around the middle of the 15th century the climate changed and it became cooler which in turn shortened the crop growth period and instances of the black death in Iceland. It can be said that the touched parts of the Danish sphere of influence were characterized by a restricted ability to move and have contacts within the framework of the world. For two hundred years of relative seclusion, dance music waned and was replaced by epic folk ballads and rhyming stanza songs for those boring winter nights.

Word/number puzzles were fun and served as thinking and memory teasers for the audiences in real-time during assembly in farmstead dwelling houses; they also provided the mode of expressing feeling through creative expressions. Satirical "nid" songs Bring rumours and scandal-mongering around the distant rural areas. There were mythic monsters that children's ballads credited as the Icelanders who have a residence in the wilderness and are still seen in the interior highlands. This beautiful folk music in question effectively bound the people of Iceland together socially after a difficult initiatory experience.

In their peculiar situation, the formation of popular music and nationalism were connected with Iceland's efforts to become an independent nation in the nineteenth century. This is because there were poets such as Jónas Hallgrímsson who made sure that contemporary lyrics calling for independence from Denmark were sung to well-understood traditional melodies and therefore spread among the people. Books and sheet music like those that we have, Íslenzk Þjóðlög/ Icelandic Folk Songs enabled the wonderful regional songs to be written down to promote pride.

The community was formed in the form of choral societies because in the past there were limited communication channels. Since the Icelanders and the Danes were getting at each other's throats in terms of inter- cultural relations, the Icelanders united in their calls for the form of a home rule system. One can mention singing societies that performed during the millennial celebration of Alþing in 1874 which led to the call for the country's autonomy as well as independence in 1944.

After the grant of autonomy in 1918 music changed even more because there were better means of transport and communications overseas. A variety of music was heard by the extended families after 1930 through musical programs on the radio. In 1906 with gramophone recordings, even those that slowly faded away were recorded and can be heard even today.

Post 1960 tourism and urbanization diluted the role of semi-urban and rural folk music branches. Folk music styles were interspersed with pop music melodies of Gangnam Style. They employed electronic studio techniques with the conventional vocals and instruments are there and this was practiced by artists like Megas, singers like Björk and bands like Sigur Rós.

Certain of the scholars who took part was Dr. Ólafur Pálmason who was a researcher and teacher of Icelandic music at the universities. Later rimur, chanting for langspil, makes sure that the public does not be bored with this type of art Musicologists begin to document new emerging regional songs in remote villages. It widened the ability of music selection and kept the folk practice active for the tourists.

From the above-mentioned issues, it can generally be understood that Icelandic folk music has its roots and is influenced by the geographical features and the historical background of Iceland which portrays a powerful strong cultural identity through its tones. This lively treeless country piece involves the use of langspil and fiddle and multipart vocal harmonies that are incorporated in this creative work. Stressing severe climate and geographical remoteness contributed to the development of a musical culture which helped strengthen the unity and the identity of Icelanders in the critical periods.

And now, living folk tradition in Iceland is combined with modernity — it is sung in the kitchen in a home, on stage at summer festivals, and through speakers into the hearts of Icelanders. This music represents the story of which Iceland is itself – isolated but creative, transient but tough, shaped by the geology but remolded by the history and civilization of eleven hundred years. This kind of ethnic music may change and remain with Icelanders today as a form of collective memory anchored on harmonic timbre to an uncertain, but hopeful future.

Themes and Practices

Folk music continues to be a component of the pop music market in the Nordic countries which include Denmark, Finland, Iceland, Norway and Sweden. However, it should be pointed out that the Nordic folk tunes were sung over a thousand years ago and are considered elements of the history, story, celebration and identity of these countries. Like with all the genres, certain general trends and tendencies are characteristic of this category.

Mythology is one of the significant components of Nordic folk music that has been preserving myths, legends and folk tales that date back to even the Vikings. Some of the songs that people have been singing for generations depict characters and incidences of Norse mythology or ancient saga. Some relate modern-day stories of heroes and the heroines, the villain, the warrior, the magician and the rest from the folk tales passed on orally. The Nordic people greatly value their oral history, and this is evidenced by the fact that most of the Nordic folk contain lyrics.

An example of this is the "Kalevala", the Finnish national epic written in the nineteenth century but drawn from the Karelian and Finnish oral literature and mythology. Of the runes of this poem most of them have been associated with different traditional folk songs. They call to Väinämöinen, a shamanistic hero, who with kantele, a Finnish zither played enchantment and performed heroic feats. As the trickster, Väinämöinen takes one passage in which he carved the first kantele from the jaw of a giant pike to win Aino, a beautiful woman in marriage through singing. Even though she kills herself rather than marrying Väinämöinen, this shaman is depicted to be playing the instrument later on. Such and many other episodes from the Kalevala have been used to produce folk songs and musical works on the mythology.

Folk narratives are also dominant in the genre of Nordic ballads. An unfortunate example is "Agnete og Havmanden" which is Danish for "Agnete and the Merman". In this Danish ballad from the nineteenth century, a young woman named Agnete turns down her lover Niels to be the wife of the merman who tells her about gold and glittering treasures in his underwater realm. But she describes life beneath the sea as dark and completely devoid of the warmth and comfort that she enjoyed on the surface. One day when she goes home to visit, her mother refuses to accept her new form of being an amphibious creature. The distressed father sees her swimming away. Thus, the plot where a woman becomes a member of a non-human partner can be considered typical for Nordic folklore, and this ballad is its embodiment.

Beowulf is one of the oldest pieces of literature, epic in form, telling the stories of the Scandinavian society. While it is older than what is nowadays understood as Nordic folk music, most scholars think that the poem was meant to be recited with music. It has certainly inspired more contemporary folk interpretations, specifically the song "Beowulf" by the acclaimed Norwegian folk band

Wardruna on their 2016 concept album based on Nordic mythology. They are examples of how the legendary history of the Norse still influences Nordic folk music up to the present day.

In general, it is crucial to mention that Nordic folk music is closely connected with narratives; narratives regarding the legends, mythology, folk tales, and histories of the region became the motivation and the matter for numerous songs inherited for generations. Thus, the song is a shared experience of listening and talking in Scandinavia, a way of remembering a fable, commemorating a Nordic god, or dramatizing the deeds of a folk hero – in all, the function of storytelling stays the same.

Music has an exceptionally important role in joyous cultural and communal festivities across the Nordic countries. These folks' tunes can be performed during the festive season for instance during Christmas, Midsummer, Easter and many other occasions. They are also useful for regional festivals which are aimed at letting people know the historical past as well as the culture of a specific area. These celebrations contribute not only to preserving the existence of Nordic folk music but also to further evolution because of the processes taking place.

Regarding the grand scale of popular dance and merrymaking of folk music, there are the major folk music festivals that have evolved in the Nordic countries since the period of the 1960s. In Denmark, the annual Tønder Festival is a festival of folk which began in the year of 1974 and is gradually gaining its place among the largest folk festivals in Europe attracting more than fifty thousand people. Owing to its interesting locations like stages, streets, and musical workshops; musicians from the Nordic countries as well as other parts of the world visit the place. Thus, although it was rooted in the traditions of a certain country, namely Denmark, the festival incorporated most of the traditional and modern kinds of folk music. In the light of Tønder, other big-scale folk festivals have been organized all across Scandinavia and Finland.

At present, Iceland has several extremely large and popular summer folk festivals, and all of them continue to play an especially important role in promulgating the image of Iceland as a country that has a very distinct and in ever composed and correspondingly distinctly isolated folk music scene, as well as in presenting the contemporary trends of the folk music movement. Folk musical pairs and groups of relatives are especially important in Icelandic folk music. Songs about forefathers hundreds of years ago in the description of Iceland are characterized by its rocky and to some extent severe landscape which affected the souls of Iceland people. Some of these profound musical cultures evidenced at Þjóðhátíð and LungA provide international tourists with the first real taste of Icelander cultures.

In the Faroe Islands, the summertime is the time of the village festivities particularly that of Ólavsøka in honor of Sankt-Olav. These celebrations last a week and therefore contain parades, dances, Children's entertainment and great and extensive Faroese food and drinks. People listen to folk musicians playing dance melodies and ballads till late in the night and the young and the elderly put on their colourful woolen garments to do the official Olavsøka dance. Although each of the island villages adds its color to the festival, together they aim at offering people reunification, safeguarding culture and traditions for the Faroese both those who live in the country and those who are in the diaspora.

While the celebration of Christmas, Midsummer, as well as Easter, is somewhat different in each of the Scandinavian countries, folk music is the unchangeable tradition in all of them. In the case of the people of Laponia in northern Norway, Sweden and Finland midsummer period is ushered in through fire light, and fast-moving songs from traditional joik singers and drummers in a parade-like celebration as they welcome the sun home. Families danced in folk costumes near the festive Midsummer poles and children recited and sang folk songs, and such folk games as Goble, Round dance, Lad's vertep, Girls' vertep, Chairs, etc. The known annual Jokkmokk winter market began at least in 1605; associated with distant towns' business with Christmas and Easter markets. Indigenous Sámi musicians and singers, craftspeople and weavers come to this rather remote area for several days of holiday trading.

Holidays as well as folk music festivals should be kept alive for preserving Nordic culture and so that the music of the region does not get stagnant. They include gathering of the youth and the elderly as they entertain each other with folklores that remind them of their roots and place. The songs make musicians keep on performing the songs of their ancestors at the same time as taking on new features of society today. Therefore, the cyclical narratives of oral continue as additional links to an exceptionally long chain.

The Pagan Nordic folk music for that matter has started from the Island, valley or village by the coast yet the inter-cultural interactions have always been an interesting eye-opener for centuries. In the matter of facts from the Viking adventures to other continents and back outside musical inputs mingled with the Nordic populations up to a certain point. One of the contributory forces that affected the development of folk music was occupation by European powers most particularly in the late medieval age. Over the past century, new opportunities in internalization and the boosted speed of diffusing musical trends globally have brought a multiethnic colour to folk music in the Nordic countries.

Drawing motifs of the sea, most of the Nordic national anthems encompass 'Norsemen' who sailed and bought goods in the longships from the Viking Age in the 8th century AD period. This is an early Europeans who became an outcome of geographical discovery and colonization of other parts by the Nordic peoples. As the mentioned historians claim, for example, Vikings borrowed rhythms, scales, instruments and styles of song singing from Spain, Siberia and the Middle East, as well as other ones, but these were associated with the native song and music of the countries which were colonized by the Vikings. These new findings of stringed musical instruments such as the Swedish Hummel, the Norwegian Langeleik and the Finnish and Sami kanteles also support the history of progressive evolution of music with such non-traditional features in the Nordic region.

In the medieval period, people sang their songs to scholars and clerics from Nordic countries to the rest of Europe as the laureates were learning from the old poetic eddas while bards performed in the royal courts across Europe. As a result, such popular melodies that contributed to Western church music and the romantic ballad look like an inspiration for the Nordic musical styles of the given period. The later key cultural event exposed new outside musical experiences to the Nordics. During the 14th century, Denmark's Queen Margaret was ruling both Norway as well as Sweden, the idea and the concept of unification as well as national integration emerged when folk tunes without much show of crossing the border of Scandinavian provinces. The following centuries witnessed plagues such as the Black Death plague, which impacted Nordic folk music in one or the other by sparking the Christian Reformation, Printing Press influence and European wars as well.

Moving forward to the twentieth century the post-war American sensual gospel jazz and rock and roll also influenced the Nordic folk songs. Using the local colour, new generations placed the cores of the blues scales, snare drums and vocal intonations to the American-Scandinavian folk melodies. Norway became popular through various artists for instance Sven Nyhus & Saft who were engaged in their own accented country blues genre. Swedish fiddlers brought 'shine' to the waltz and light footedness to the Swedish dance and applied it to the brass slide and the swing beats of the Appalachians. The Danish singers; Povl Dissing and Tamra

Rosanes were also part of a rather opulent folk movement, coming from the Nordic countries but connected more to the American folk movement icons like Pete Seeger and Woody Guthrie, yet deeply rooted in Nordic folk and fairy tales sung in the vernacular.

And when all types of music were again given a greater push in the international domain due to the progression of electronic media technologies in the new millennium, Nordic folk bands also incorporated other more diverse ethnic styles of music from worldwide like Spanish flamenco, Brazilian Tropicalia, Afro Caribbean reggae, Algerian Rai, Ghanian highlife, Mongolian folk metal and other. Even as this culturally unbounded experimentation has led the Nordic folk umbrella so far away from the folk in reality, this commitment is still in theory to community, nature and tradition.

Thus, if one were to take a broader perspective in looking across the continuum of evolution, Nordic folk music can be best characterized not by the degree of its pure, unadulterated longevity in isolation but more fundamentally by spirit and place ever changes. It is then permitted to absorb foreign input as a woolen tunic yet remains well-defined and has not lost its identity. In contemporary times, globalization has endearably extended the perimeters of Nordic folk music possibility into infinity. But it is still a matter of core, even if it is now polished, digitized, or fused, the heart that still beats as a heathen hearth calling to mind the snow-blanketed northern forests and the silent waters of the fjords that first stirred the Nordic tongues centuries ago.

With folk music of the Nordic countries as the foundation, soundtracks of many fabulous and essential fantastic and adventurous motion pictures are in demand. This, however, for Shore, who was the composer of the Lord of the Rings, meant that he had to familiarize himself with Scandinavian tunes and incorporate these into the final soundtracks. The choral moments and the use of likely folk-string orchestration point and nod toward the mythos of its Scandinavian roots. The Lord of the Rings vocal themes are sung by Enya who blended her enchanting tracks with a tinge of traces of Nordic. Soft and touching timbre, a hint of drama in her voice, mournful violins, and deep reflection of great bass drums set the mystical and rather eerie tone of the film's settings.

Like the music in Tangled, a considerable amount of power in the music that underwrites

Frozen comes from the Nordic musical motifs. The songs are closer to, for example, the songs from musicals such as those on Broadway, but parts of the music and the chorus originate from fiddle tunes and Sámi and Scandinavian chanting. These hints of the Nordic are included together with the aspects of triumph; the utmost emphasis on the basic features of the environments of the frozen areas. The other elements that the global audiences responded to were the pervasive characters and the empowering themes which paved the two that paved way for the second wave of appreciation of Nordic themes.

In the historical drama television show Vikings, the metal and mixed compositions including goat horns, frame drums, lyres, and lur horns that were in use by the Norse and the Celts are used in the activity scenes. These are deep, leathery instruments and the audience expects the savageness of the Viking fighters; they also think of them as means to communicate with the gods and the ground. Melodious pentatonic hooks repeat the emotions of loneliness that Scandinavia wilds with an occasional powerful drumming keeping the rhythm as while rowing a boat. Thus, this raw score increases the characters' psychological tensions and inner struggles.

However, these folks' influences are not only in the fantasy and historical-themed movies, they show up where one would least expect to see them such as in The Muppets' Christmas special. Here the characters join their hand and sing a happy Finn's dance song in the middle of the snowy forest one could imagine from a Finnish fairy tale movie. Mellow glockenspiels adorn melody line five tunes and joyful mandolins. Subsection is the ultimate reflection of the element of a clean and closely-knit village which forms a major part of all the folk music from the Nordic region.

In recent centuries many books and other types of literature have also incorporated aspects of Nordic mythology with music. Such an instance to refer to is the young J. R. R. Tolkien whose work was enriched a lot by the Old Norse language and mythology that he studied. The author also remains an heir of the Nordic epics in his novels. The dwarves in the shatterdose of mythological undertakers of the German and its popular tales the elf languages are a concoction created from the Icelandic and Finnish languages and their semantics. And therefore, Middle Earth, where everything happens, looks like the Scandinavians' lands and accepts their principal values.

The fact that she worked in the age of nineteenth century, which is defined as the age of Nordic romantic nationalism, has not prevented her fairy tales from being enjoyed all around the world as children's books. These are stories like 'The Snow Queen' and 'The Little Mermaid' and the story of 'Steadfast Tin Soldier' are drenched with Denmark out of snow, rock, toys, and lonely characters representing the face of the Nordic spirit. Elements of these stories have been taken and used in several animated and live-action films, numbering in the dozens.

With academic air but in the nineteenth century Elias Lönnrot is famous for creating and publishing the Finnish and Karelian oral poetry epic called Kalevala which has mythic songs and stories in it. Even though this poetic cycle preserves historical data of tremendous worth, it has also encouraged creativity in other artists. Not only the meter of the Kalevala but also this matter was to directly impact writers such as Tolkien and musicians like Sibelius starting from metal bands, Enslaved to cartoons and Might Thor comic series.

Besides cinema and fairy tales, the Nordic elements have penetrated different kinds of contemporary upgrade musicians, including indie folk & country, occult heavy metal and others.

Värttinä and Gjallarhorn started in the nineties and organized the renewal of the interest in Nordic folk music with apocalyptic and hi-tech images. Their raw string orchestrations and voice harmonization provided messengers of the past scholarly wisdom and the current technology. This consequence was great for many ambient electronic and Neo-folk artists and the works of the Wardruna and Danheim are a great example; using the elements of Norse instruments with tribal beat and ethereal vocals. They told me they're making ritual music and they wish to infuse it with the spirit of Vikings from several centuries back.

But even the country-pop star Taylor Swift, who sings more into the mainstream, referred to her Scandinavian roots by releasing the Folklore album in 2020. The album seems to broadcast a flagrantly rustic, arboreal message, heroic tones and calls to principal motifs and regular motifs from Scandinavia. To start with, Swift increased the number of touring bands and included musicians from Scandinavian folk bands to her previously rather personal pop songs.

Not only atmospheric and acoustic styles of the region, but also nuer_myk jord the harder rocking foods of the Nordic folk. The beat on "Immigrant Song" with Led Zeppelin can only be described as the timpani and the ululations literally the type that is heard in the literature related to Viking invasions. One of the latest examples might be Draconian – a Swedish doom metal band in which female classically trained vocalists perform sad Gothic poetry accompanied by heavy strings and metals. In terms of their work, they can bear a distant relation to the Nordic folk dirges but as for visual and aesthetic appeal, these dolls are more similar to funerals.

Another example of this rather typical Nordic kind of formula is the Indie folk troupe Of Monsters and Men, which equally emerged from the streaming services and some strange corners of the social media genre to the mainstream. This is a clear indication of how acts from the Nordic countries with folk influences are no longer enclosed by cultural barriers hence helping change new generations across the world. Their shouted gang choruses and drunken rock and roll hysteria are heartfelt but they are also fun.

These few examples indicate how one can still find Nordic folk creeping into apparently unrelated art forms are numerous. The rawness and the mythology of Nordic folk music are still fresh as it is translated to other means of art and help viewers to be transcendent to other dimensions of life.

Of course, Nordic folk constitutes one of the fundamental pillars supporting the general

Nordic pop culture delivering, some refer to as Nordic creative renaissance in the fields of design, food, literature, television and much more. Nordic creators incorporate history and genuine compassion into their creations. Folk music thus captures core features of this Nordic frame of mind that continues to disseminate creativity in all directions, like expanding circles in a frozen lake. People worldwide resonate with a clean, wholesome, and profound experience that Nordic creative representation brings back to the homeland, which is rooted in folk art from undetermined generations under the aurora borealis.

Hence, while there is a never-ending list of new media works influenced by Nordic, it is only advised to also look for primary folk sources that are still preserved by enthusiasts who honor these deep and powerful traditions irrespective of the changes that trends bring.

Thus, by supporting grassroots culture keepers, we maintain creative fires that will carry on fueling the imagination of the masses through all the future media yet to emerge.

The Future

Consequently, the foundation for the sounds of many groups and styles has originated in the traditional folk instruments of the Nordic countries along with their rhythms and songs, but in the last decades there have appeared several fusions with other contemporary genres. Today more and more artists from Nordic countries are using pop, rock, jazz, electronic and even metal in new reels, ballads, polskas & waltzes. There has been a shift to folk-pop after this has been able to succeed in appealing to the young people of the country and also in popularizing Norwegian folk tunes across the globe.

Some of the most popular contemporary Nordic folk fusion genres include, among the numerous contemporary Nordic folk fusion concepts it is possible to distinguish:

Folk Metal: On this record, the only acoustic instruments included in songs are microphones and folk instruments accompanied by fast metal guitar, drums, and harsh vocals. Emerging from the Finnish band Finn troll in the early 1990s, the characteristic Nordic folk metal prevails in Nordic countries and partially in Eastern Europe with the majority of the Metal lyrics inspired from Norse mythology or folklore.

Nordicana: Interpretations of the Northern Europe traditional music with elements of roots and traditional American music. Well, besides the traditional country music instruments such as fiddles and woodwinds, there is also the use of pedal steel and banjos that create a down and almost lonely feeling of Nordicana. A few of them are Norwegian singer and songwriter, Ane Brun as well as Danish indie rock band named The William Blakes.

Electro Folk: There are the sounds of Nordic folk in electronic, synth and dance music. Of Monsters and Men, the neo-folk band from Iceland and the electro-folk came to mainstream popularity in early 2010; the First Aid Kit is another Swedish duo making Nordic folk music with a recent addition of electronic components into their music.

Each of these modern hybrids preserves certain references to the per-Nordic baroque musical background of the seventeenth century or earlier, and it incorporates two novelties: the use of amplification and electronic manipulation. The mutual reinforcement of tradition and innovation has proven to have been the key to the growth of Nordic folk music in the twenty-first century.

Besides, the constantly increasing popularity of Nordic folk music in the 21st century has also greatly relied on adopting new technologies. Currently many artists in the Nordic folk genre have been benefiting from new trends in music distribution, specifically from digital media such as Spotify, YouTube, and SoundCloud, among others. It has also cemented the social and commercial relations between those fans of Nordic folk music who would otherwise be separated by a distance of miles and kilometres.

The overall numbers of the digital distribution as well as the streaming also validate the idea of the dramatic growth of the popularity of Nordic folk music. For instance, First Aid Kit which is an American folk duo increased monthly listeners in Spotify from 200000 to more than 5 million between 2010 and 2022. Independent Norwegian folk singer Aurora moved from almost completely unknown to having more than one million listeners in the month following the release of her first album in 2015. It therefore shows that digital access also provides an opportunity to other unknown listeners of Nordic folk music.

The following are how technology has impacted on the production of the Nordic folk music. The acoustic instruments are still being used but the nuances such as amplifiers, effects pedals, synthesized beats and computer-aided mixing and mastering of the album have altered the music's timbres.

Since drummers who can play for many Finnish folk metal bands, including Korpiklaani, are difficult to find, the bands use loud distortion guitars and digital drums; the timing is written by computer programmers. In digitized studio, Aurora, the singer-songwriter layers rich vocal harmonies and keyboard beds with overdubs. All these sounds cannot be produced without today's modern tools of recording and production.

On the other hand, algorithms proposing Scandinavian folk styles have also brought about new listens to classical micro-styles.

What might be considered quite remarkable, however, is the fact that by the final ten years of the twentieth-century technology can cast light on such nicety as modern fusion as well as the old traditional Nordic folk music.

New generations have also adopted it, elder musicians of the Nordic folk are still passing their knowledge to the younger musicians and at the same time young artists are also helping the music to go in new directions. What young talents add to the art' source with the perception of the modern world and, at the same time, indicate the enhanced focus on the Nordic background, as well as achieving a balance between tradition and innovation.

New trends as follows are rapping in the ancient language of Scandinavia, off-stage participation of ethnic musicians in the band, modern attitude to sexual orientation in the text, and expressing a social-political opinion on social evils including global warming. Some representative examples include:

- Árstíðir is an Icelandic folk rapper who incorporates traditional Icelandic Rímur with other modern genres like rap, hip- hop; Árstíðir delivers his lines in Old Norse. He wears medieval costumes in his music videos and so he relates early poetry to today's music production.

- The Norwegian singer Moddi expanded a hard rock campaign to the Nordic folk ballad "Troll Rock "and the reference to right-wing extremism. Other songs are about issues like homelessness and the deteriorating environment therefore can equally sing the song on behalf of folk music making a statement about the society.

- The instruments thereof are the djembe drums from West Africa, the Arabic stringed instrument, the oud together with the Scandinavian fiddles as well as flutes. They are all of mixed ages and ethnic backgrounds, in this way, their approach is progressive and multicultural coming from Nordic countries but inherited folk traditions.

It is now possible to speak about young Nordic artists who are not only improvising but reintroducing traditions, as well. Moddi may rap in old dialects while turning up aggressive electric guitars but the fact that poetry from ages can still be heard in the present day makes the difference. That is why it appears to be interesting for young people from all over the world that the Nordic folk had an opportunity to keep their ancient legacy and evolve to make it appropriate for the present society.

The first problem is that young musicians of the Nordic countries do not have models of tradition-bearers and genuine performers of folk songs. One might get the impression that with the death of the older generation performers, there is no one to replace them among the young people. The disruption in this tradition where it is passed on from one generation to another poses continuity of Nordic folk music traditions. But even if the youth learns folk music today, he or she will not be able to feel people who used to practice it, which will undoubtedly influence some styles of living.

Increased standardization of Nordic folk music and additional commercialization likewise present the danger of the further erosion of sub-genres and regional special, and unique styles of this music. With increased interaction in the present-day world than before, the blend of the folk music traditions inherent in the isolated people is reducing. Therefore, certain specific genres related to certain specific locations in the Nordic may thus become useless. The provision of only main versions also creates more standardization rather than diversification being experienced in other platforms.

However, the documenting and academician of Nordic folk music poses some problems, because the type of music that was in circulation was 'word of mouth only', and there were no written works or detailed records of the music which was being produced. But, there are some albums and books on Nordic folk songs at present and they are not many as part of the Northern European traditional music. The latter is true in the sense that localized aspects of folk music; and variations in music produced in one context as compared to another are not described in detail. When musicians pass on, their songs that have not been documented are consigned to the dustbin hence there is a loss of knowledge.

The relationship with folk music and languages across the Nordic region further makes it challenging when it comes to preservation. The Sami people of Northern Norway, Sweden, and Finland traditionally have had the joik songs as being among the usages of their native people group. However, recently, young people who speak Sami have been dwindling which means that they do not spread joiks to the new young generation. Similarly, the less common and the most threatened regional idioms of the North Germanic languages also pose problems regarding the folk songs that are embedded in the corresponding languages.

However, there are a few issues that have emerged together with the new opportunities for further development of a passion for Nordic folk arts. Modern techniques in recording and better mass media and the internet contribute to the strengthening and acknowledgment of Nordic folk music. This is the case of Nordic folk performers who use outlets like Spotify to increase their sales. As for such practices as kulning – the Swedish herding calls, one can turn to YouTube, blogs, and forums that connect people all over the world and spark their interest in Nordic folk music. Technology is used to further break the boundaries of reaching more people and also expand the possibilities of creativity that are present within traditions.

Generally, these Nordic folk motifs have also been incorporated into popular music and culture in the recent past and therefore have made the youth embrace them again. For example, the Danish Nordicana genre unites Americana music with the folk of Nordic or Swedish folk-pop which integrates the traditional Nordic style with English pop music. These popular renditions inspired by folk music both broaden the audience's perception of the extraordinary musical genre and help reawaken the young generations of native people of the Nordic countries. It is equally assertive in developing dialogue with the people outside whilst retaining continuity from Aboriginal roots.

This cross-pollination also results in the possibility of the formation of new inter-genre projects that comprise musicians from the Nordic region and other parts of the world. For instance, Songlines Scandinavia fuses some aspects of the north of Europe folk and Jazz and Symphonic and world music. It also adds instruments like the West African kora when playing with the Turkish Sufi musicians as well as the Indian classical vocals when mixed with the Chinese sheng. In this way, creative exchanges create international partnerships that could be used for popularizing Nordic folk music by relating it to a huge musical space. The opportunities are in changing the culture of solitude with the culture of interculturality.

Furthermore, students in universities and faculties of several Nordic nations and other parts of the world engage in numerous research activities, academic seminars and cultural interchanges related to Nordic folk music. This is why ethnomusicology programs have focused significant attention on the promotion of awareness of Nordic folk traditions around the world. The Nordic embassies and cultural institutes also promote and educate people globally about the folk music and instruments of their country through the concerts, workshops, and lecture demonstrations. Such academic endeavors contribute to the development of ethnomusicology and the understanding of Nordic forms in the global academia.

Starting from the historical Nordic campaigns by intellectuals and cultural nationalists and moving up to the creation of the folk music archival institutions in the present, constant endeavors have sustained the renaissance and preservation of Nordic folk traditions despite the increasing threats of modernization. They also respond to some of the challenges which are faced by the tradition bearers.

It is only logical that the efforts toward the preservation of Nordic folk music started as early as in late 18th century when European Romantic-era scholars started calling for more extensive and systematic efforts in terms of documenting, researching and publishing traditional Nordic folk songs. Linguistic folk heritage was saved by people like Danish priest N.S.F. Grundtvig, and musicians such as Edvard Grieg and Carl Nielsen who traveled across the country, collecting hundreds if not thousands of old folk songs from peasants and farmers – for hundreds of which were later recorded and turned into classical music pieces. It enhanced their fieldwork about Nordic folk music which enriched the academic study of the particular subject.

Much later in the 20th century the Swedish Folk Music Research Department and the Norwegian Institute for Comparative Folk Music Research began formal preservation campaigns. Other countries like Finland, Sweden and Denmark also established state-funded folk music archives to collect recordings and documents of all the genres and styles that came up in the country. Such institutional impartations were supplemented by private NGOs such as the Association for the Preservation and Cultivation of Danish Folk Music.

Various government policies also contributed towards folk music revival for instance the

Denmark Radio channel for which there were specific slots in a week dedicated to folk music shows. Festivals like the Kaustinen Folk Music Festival that began in the year 1968 began to provide performance space for folk artists, especially for young talents. After 2006, Árni Magnússon Institute in Iceland restored and archived old Iceland including folk music recordings from the 1930s.

Therefore, even today the countries of the North preserve the support of preservation profiles through cultural policies and have kept traditional music education in schools. For instance, there is a Norwegian institution named Ole Bull Academy that is dedicated to violation education grounded on Hardanger fiddling. The contemporary entitativity of Denmark which is the last action plan indicates that the Ministry of Culture would be expected to fund fieldwork on the diversity of folkloristic activities in the country. The plan also plans to use folk music to prevent rising cultural division within the minority Danish population which has become rampant.

Apart from the governmental campaigns conducted by each country's government, some movements are run from the bottom up that help in preservation across all the Nordic countries. Some of the riksspelman music unions in Sweden include the having tens of thousands of fiddler members for instance they have organized events to share the Swedish folk styles among fellows. This is a work that some of the more amateur cultural bearings such as the Norwegian Bygdelag associations try to do to retain the popular arts that come from specific rural districts among the urban dwellers.

These include ethnical Non-Governmental Organisations like the Society for the Promotion of Finnish Sami Culture in Helsinki or the Sami Artist Group in Norway which popularize the Lappish Sami cultural aspect through either a workshop or an arts display. Other examples of such a local Nordic group are Iceland's, grassroots group Miðaldamót performing medieval Icelandic folk music in both countries and other countries including their foreign tours dressed in medieval costumes. To sum up, the non-institutional organizations build up the defenselessness of the appropriation of Nordic people's culture.

Of greater significance was the late nineteenth/ early twentieth centuries Nordic folk revivalist campaigns which created patriotic pride in indigenous music, as a cultural icon against Americanization. Grieg like other composers who brought folk tunes to the center of development in musical forms changed folk music into a national culture in Norway hence urging generations to follow.

Even the later mainstream pop and rock bands were influenced by it sending such new-age Nordic folk bands, which appeared in Sweden in the second half of the 1980s including Hedningarna and Groupa, into world music. Danish doom folk persona Myrkur by Amalie Bruun and dark folk groups such as Of the Wand and Moon from Denmark make Paganism appealing to the young generation of the world with ethnic passion once in a while. They popularise folk through the world music Market so that the young people appreciate their indigenous cultures.

It is possible to pinpoint a few rather evident trends in Nordic folk, which can give certain hints regarding the nature of its evolution. First of all, it has gone beyond the limits and gained an audience from different countries and collaborated with such directions as world and folktronica music. Other convinces of the gradually increasing popularity of this genre are such international collaborations as Trio Mio from Denmark trying Middle Eastern inflection or First Aid Kit from Sweden recording with American indie folk artists. This fusion with other styles also aims at more and young people. The current performers of folktronica music including the Norwegians of Glittertind who meld folk with modern electronics may be utilizing a nerdy methodology to reach future fans.

Second, contemporary bands are changing their practices concerning song productions and presentations. Various groups including Finland's Frigg participate in building new orchestration formations that are not dictated by prescriptions of conventionality. These fiddle/ flute/ guitar/ bass/ percussion pieces, combined with occasional beatbox, and excellent utilized vocal harmonies bring a modern sound, but still very characteristic for the Nordic countries. It provides folk music with new tones that are suitable for twenty-first-century fashion.

Last but not least is entertainment, and the change in the genre is from entertainment to art. While once Nordic folk might represent regional life and culture, today it covers social and political issues ranging from climate change to refugees, and women's rights. Kings & Fools from Norway combine the roots of traditional folk music with topical themes in their lyrics or at least they try to while First Aid Kit, sisters from Sweden, use the foundations of folk ballads as a base for reflecting on modern women. This socially conscious twist goes far in aiding relevancy because people are seeking music with messages in their ears more and more.

Tantalizing hybridization may attract more listeners who are open to this new type of music but Nordic purists worry that it will lose that core traditional Nordic folk voice if it goes off the tracks. That does not mean that we do not have to preserve the heritage because the two goals have to be achieved, but not at the expense of others. Sustaining indigenous and local artists and folk music guarantees Nordic originality and staples while nurturing up-and-coming artists and groups. Governments may sponsor and contribute research in archives and ethnomusicology as well as contribute and sustain cultural actions and movements acting as shields from globalization. Newspaper, radio and television also air folk music both nationally and internationally while musical fairs such as Sweden's Folk och Världsmusik and Norwegian Folklore are also other annual celebrations of traditional and contemporary Nordic folk.

The other is education which refers to the level of formal learning that an individual has undergone. Folk music as a part of the school curriculum extends its information further, allowing learners to master such instruments as the nyckelharpa or willow flute and to study dances of the North. For instance, the Royal College of Music in Stockholm is aimed at enhancing the ICT skills of young professionals and future-generation carriers. While developing this kind of genre, we must remember that certain elements of its prerequisites as the geographic cultural identity should be saved.

By its predisposition, folk music was and remains one of the most socially oriented musical phenomena that is organically set in the given space. It can then become made more accessible for such a participatory spirit to be sustained. The active participation of folk from different fields like design, dance, and theatre among others provides new scenarios in which it can be performed. Swedish fashion company ACNE, to release folk influenced collection worked with artists and also integrated Nordic design into urban outfits. In Iceland, the folk dance ensemble ILLSKA used old steps and costumes in staged concerts and performances. People of all sorts, even restaurants hire folk bands for instance the Geranium restaurant that is located in Copenhagen was found to have special evenings that featured Bornholm island dishes and songs. Such creativity and interdisciplinary reach thus offer more options of the commercial consumers for regional culture while developing local talents.

Society, through the use of different platforms in social networks, is a huge opportunity for the further development of folk music in the countries of the Nordic. Streaming is an innovative method of distribution and big data includes information on targeting a new customer base. Some ways through which the genre is marketed to such other audiences include recommended playlists of folk music from Nordic countries as 'Best of Nordic Folk' on Spotify, Pandora as well as YouTube. It also brings Nordic folk fusion bands to the fans of the world, indie pop, and folktronica when recommending these bands together with other more distant genres using algorithms.

Creative cooperation takes place on the Web. Chromatic tuner of the Finnish music application Yousician facilitates traditional instrument learning while Sweden-born Ohmni includes backing tracks and sheet music for learners. On social media, the hashtags help to unite the scattered fans so that they can interact irrespective of the country they belong to. Digital adaptation discovers the actual concerts and remains connected with the generations that are predominantly digital.

Besides, one can come across possible virtual folk bands as well as avatars. Future generations might be able to attend concerts of their favorite groups or bands, in hologram form or persons in the afterlife may be projected as holograms. Now Live performances of South Korean pop bands are performing the autographs as augmented reality concerts and 3D avatars. Therefore, as metaverse environments will grow we might see digitalized Nordic folk stars. This is where the physicality of music meets the innovative core, as folk Nordic is set to carry the latter's progressive spirit.

It is therefore necessary that the next generations are interested in setting precursors where the objects as such may appeal emotionally. Because Nordic folk is about the feeling of the space and warmth that is linked with this snowy context, it is essential to mix the Twentieth century with the primeval nature of the North. In other words, artists have to continue to incarnate the charming uncontaminated forests, the mountains, and the silent fjords of this country through avant-garde media. Norwegian singer Aurora is a perfect example of this and she sings traditional folk music and mixes it into catchy pop music which couldn't be any more 'Nordic' if you tried, add in her ethereal polar night vocals and her lyrics about the mythical north. From a village fire to modern streaming services, the authenticity has to go on touching people's hearts and minds.

Thus, the transition of music from the Nordic countries from a cultural product to a global one will be shaped by the pioneers and the precursors. Original pioneers lead change without replacing the spirit with the purpose of innovative change realignments. Henceforth, if one would apply rightful levels of creativity along with adequate planning and contacts in social networks, perhaps quaint Scandinavian folk art would last for generations. Despite taking a pessimistic view of the prospects of the projects, it is still possible to keep a positive outlook on the subject of further development of Nordic folklore. As long as the skies shine with northern lights and pines covered with snow, the music of this region and the words in it will continue to sing in the future music.

Disclaimer

Everything shared in this book should be considered as educational and informative in nature. The author and publisher shall not be responsible for any loss or damage suffered by any reader directly or indirectly through reading of, reliance on, and use of information that only the author and the publisher know at the time of writing this book.

Some of the suggestions given and the approaches recommended in the book may not be applicable to certain circumstances. The author and the publisher shall not be held responsible for any damages caused as a direct result of the use or non-use of the information presented in this book.

It is understood that readers should not rely on it for professional solicitations such as medical, legal, financial, and other related opinions. If any professional help is needed, then advice of a competent professional person should be taken.

The author and the publisher will not be held responsible for direct, indirect, special, or consequential damages or any other costs whatsoever arising from the use of the information present herein in this book.

About the Author

Maher Asaad Baker (In Arabic: ماهر أسعد بكر), is a Syrian musician, author, journalist, VFX & graphic artist, and director. He was born in Damascus in 1977. He grew up with a dream of being one of the most well-known artists in the world, and he has been working hard to achieve it ever since.

He started his career in 1997 when he was only 20 years old. He had a passion for technology and media, and he taught himself how to develop applications and websites. He also explored various types of media-creating paths, such as music production, graphic design, video editing, animation, and filmmaking. He was not satisfied with just being a consumer of media; he wanted to be a creator of media.

Reading was another source of inspiration for him. He was always surrounded by books as a child, thanks to his father's extensive library. He read books from different genres, topics, and perspectives. He read books for knowledge, for wisdom, for entertainment, for enlightenment. Reading stimulated his imagination and curiosity. Reading also developed his writing skills.

He did not start writing professionally until later in his life, as he was busy with other projects and pursuits. But when he did start writing, he proved himself to be a talented and prolific writer. He wrote articles for various newspapers and magazines on topics such as politics, culture, society, art, technology, and more. He wrote books that were informative and insightful. He wrote books that were creative and captivating. He wrote books that were best-selling and award-winning.

He is most known for his book "How I wrote a million Wikipedia articles", where he shares his experience of being one of the most prolific contributors to the online encyclopedia. He reveals his methods, techniques, strategies, and secrets of writing high-quality articles on any subject in record time. He also discusses the benefits and challenges of being a Wikipedia editor in the age of information overload.

He is also known for his novel "Becoming the man", where he tells the story of a young man who goes through a series of transformations in his life. The novel explores themes such as identity, masculinity, self-discovery, love, loss, and redemption. The novel is based on his journey to becoming who he is today.

Copyright © 2024 Maher Asaad Baker